WALL COVERINGS

PANELING · WALLPAPERING · FABRICS · PAINTING

**By the Editors
of Sunset Books
and Sunset Magazine**

Soft, Subtle, and Sensational
Soothing shades of violet and blue paint highlight colors in furnishings and make the room seem larger. The look is polished and contemporary. Design: Osburn Design.

LANE PUBLISHING CO. · MENLO PARK, CALIFORNIA

Details Count
Wallpaper pattern flows uninterrupted over a switch faceplate for a perfect finishing touch. Matching the pattern precisely is the key to professional effect. Design: Glenna Cook Interiors.

For professional results...

Bedroom or bath, playroom or kitchen—every room in your home needs its own special dose of color, pattern, and texture. Whether you're looking for subdued warmth in a study, romantic softness in a bedroom, or a bold burst of color for a youngster's domain, wall coverings will play an important role.

If you're on the lookout for new wall covering ideas and clear how-to instructions for applying those coverings—from wallpaper to fabric to paint to paneling—*Wall Coverings* is just the book you need. The opening chapter contains a full-color gallery of design ideas, illustrating the many uses of those four basic materials. Following are chapters devoted to step-by-step procedures—from wall preparation through installation, including how to care for your wall covering.

We extend special thanks to the following for their generosity in sharing experience and knowledge with us: Chaney's Paint & Wallcovering, Craig's Paint & Wallpaper, Poppy Fabric, The National Paint & Coatings Association, Olga Rackovich, Liddy Schmidt and Linda Kilgore, Nancy Straley, and Donald W. Vandervort.

Editor, Sunset Books: David E. Clark

Fourth printing June 1986

Edited by Alice Rich Hallowell

Photo Editor: **JoAnn Masaoka**

Design: **Joe di Chiarro**

Illustrations: **Sally Shimizu**

Cover: Photograph by **Stephen Marley**. Design by **JoAnn Masaoka**.

Photographers

Edward B. Bigelow: 17 bottom. **Jack McDowell:** 9 bottom right, 10 bottom, 11 top left & right, 13 left, 20 right, 21 right, 23 top left, 24 top, 26 top, 29 right, 30, 31. **Stephen Marley:** 4, 5, 6 top, 8, 12 right, 13 right, 15, 23 top right, 28 right, 32. **Darrow M. Watt:** 27 top. **Tom Wyatt:** 1, 2, 3, 6 bottom, 7, 9 left & top right, 10 top, 11 bottom, 12 left, 14, 16, 17 top, 18, 19, 20 left, 21 left, 22, 23 bottom, 24 bottom, 25, 26 bottom, 27 bottom left & right, 28 left, 29 left.

CONTENTS

Decorative Flair
In a quandary about what to do with outdated bathroom tiles? Picking up their color with a contemporary pattern is one answer. A border print accents the design and outlines the edges, giving tiles a custom look. Design: Jane Hartley.

GALLERY OF IDEAS

WALL COVERINGS THAT WORK

Rugged wood, soft fabric, bold prints, subtle color—which wall treatment will work best for you? Whether you're moving into a new home, remodeling an old one, or just trying to freshen up the rooms you have, you may find that you're great at organizing a room's furnishings, but lost when it comes to making the most of the walls.

Here's your chance to study many different wall coverings in a wide variety of applications. Examine the designs for color, texture, and pattern, and think about what makes each successful. Then use the ideas as springboards for creating the design most appropriate to your needs, life style, budget, and taste.

Wallpaper, fabric, paint, and paneling are all represented in this chapter. Even if you have a specific wall covering in mind, you'll find sensational variations that may be just the touch you need to turn the ordinary into the extraordinary.

Virtuoso Performance
Texture's the message conveyed in these rooms. Paneling in den (above) adds dimension and rugged warmth to a cozy retreat. Design: Michael Taylor. Refined yet inviting, hemp grasscloth adorns walls and ceiling of music room (right). White shelving defines lines and design. Design: Ruth Soforenko Associates.

WALLPAPER

Express Yourself with Pattern

Pastels on Parade

Relaxing is easy in the midst of pastel color splashes. Carried by soft breezes, flowers float across wallpaper and chaise fabric for allover effect. Fabric is treated with a coating that repels stains and water, allowing easy enjoyment. Design: Janet Nelson.

Pure and Simple

Grid pattern's crisp, clean lines uncomplicate a background, entice guests to linger in cheerful, hospitable environment. Design: Jean Chappell Interiors.

Soft as a Sigh

Delicate flower print framed by painted moldings casts a romantic spell; country-style antiques and softly draped curtains provide touches of informality and personality. The parts work together to produce an inviting combination of color, pattern, and style. Design: Nancy Bostwick.

Winning Lines

Airy, traditional pattern continuing up the wall and across the ceiling emphasizes architectural details. Fabric and handpainted floor tiles echo the pattern for blue-ribbon results. Design: Nancy Bostwick.

. . . WALLPAPER
Relative Combinations

Reflections
Coordinated stripe and floral wallpaper prints, repeated in their fabric counterparts on comforter and draperies, add royal splendor to a bedroom. Accents of soft colors and textures complete the composition. Design: Suzanne Mantell.

Family Traits
Related by color and design, patterns combine to give a bathroom distinctive elegance. Border strips emphasize the room's lines, including the unusual curve in a wall. Design: Ruth Soforenko Associates.

Double Vision
Harmonious design employs identical wallpaper and fabric prints to achieve a pretty look of pattern and line. Design: Phyllis Dunstan.

Kid-pleasing Color
Complementary colors in a petite wallpaper print are brightly repeated in fabrics and paint. Whimsical treatment relates the patterns through color, winning a youngster's heart. Design: The Cotton Works.

...WALLPAPER
The Textured Look

Bold Lines
Dark background paper dramatically highlights the knots, slubs, and hand-weaving variations of wide bark strands. Because it's woven, grasscloth can't be matched at the seams, but the effect is part of its natural beauty. Design: Trilogy Antiques & Interiors.

Refined Texture
Gracing these walls is grasscloth so fine it looks like silk. Soft shading and texture add distinction and provide a rich background for formal furnishings and art objects. Design: Jean Chappell Interiors.

Built-in Durability
Setting the stage for an ethnic art collection, "grasscloth" is really all-vinyl simulation. Rugged design combines beauty and durability in one smart product. Design: Minty Robinson.

Ethnic Accents
Handspun yarns in vertical succession make a decorative wallpaper that's functional as well. Texture and acoustic qualities were principal reasons for wallpaper selection. Paint applied later added durability.

For Discriminating Tastes
Natural color variation of wool yarns creates a warm, sophisticated wall covering. Its luxurious appearance and soft texture show off prized possessions. Design: Marc Miyasato.

. . . WALLPAPER
Showcase Appearances

Bright, Bold Approach
Lively floral print on walls and ceiling perks up a kitchen. Cheery and light-hearted, wallpaper brings the outdoors into a hard-working area. Design: Phillip Emminger.

Statement in Stripes
Vertical stripes define architectural lines and counteract the visually lowering effect of dark wood beams. Deep blue print has a touch of brown in the stripe, pulling the room's elements together. White background keeps the overall look open and airy. Design: Glenna Cook Interiors.

Eastern Tranquility
Textured grasscloth sets the stage for dramatic interplay of red and black bath accessories and oriental treasures. Wall covering only looks delicate; specially treated for water repellency, it's tough and functional. Slatted wood shelving reinforces a natural, light feeling. Design: Ruth Soforenko Associates.

Cut Down to Size
Colorful border brings a sky-high ceiling down to a manageable level for a little boy's world. Wallpaper below the border aids the deception. Design: Delsa Ham.

WALLPAPER IDEAS **13**

FABRIC
Simple Solutions

Poetic Inspiration
Charming country prints and canvas-covered walls bring a look of summer into a bedroom. Hanging length of canvas sideways on walls eliminated the need for seams, making application simple. Fabric border glued to curved molding covers staples and raw edges of canvas. Effectively placed, the border accents roof angles and continues through shirred curtains. Design: Carol Barnes/Gigi Green Interiors.

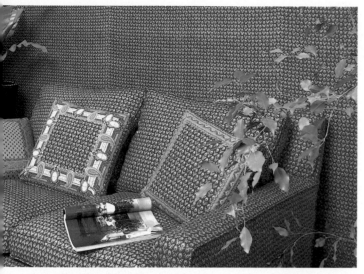

Encore
Identical pattern on walls and love seat fills the eye with color, produces a captivating setting. Seams disappear with allover print. Fabric's softness and warmth make this a cozy corner. Design: Corinne Wiley.

Orchestrated Elegance
Fabric's dark color and simple pattern warmly combine the room's elements in harmonious design. Stapled walls go up quickly, yield marvelous results. Design: In Material.

Dinner for Two
Hung in an instant, shirred walls enclose space with texture and warmth. They're practical as well, acting as insulators and sound absorbers. Design: Selby House.

. . . FABRIC
Flirting with Fabric

Plaid Personality
Square room displays individuality with
plaid fabric walls, creating a guest room
that's appealingly distinctive.
Upholstered walls: Nancy Straley.

Dream Maker
Pastel stripes float from upholstered
walls to shades and cushions. Subtle
paint color and casual furniture soften
the room, creating a cozy retreat for
daydreaming. Design/Upholstered
walls: Anthony Vella.

Regal Signature
Open enough to add light to room, regal enough to add splendor, upholstered fabric walls extend a royal welcome. Design/Upholstered walls: Anthony Vella.

Milles Fleurs
In country French style, a cheery flower print graces upholstered walls and draperies in unbroken rhythm. Coordinating fabric and border prints elegantly complete the look. Design: Martha Baum and Sharon Marston.

. . . FABRIC

Personal Expressions

Dramatic Impressions
Vibrant and exotic, shirred fabric sets a room's tone without overwhelming a special piece of art. Design: Marc Miyasato.

Distinguished Formality
Yellow moire fabric serves as a formal background for an art collection, effectively highlighting the room's architectural features at the same time. Design: Marc Miyasato.

Professional Touch

Added to muffle sound, upholstered fabric walls transformed a cold, echoing room into a warm and livable one. Wainscoting and molding elegantly complement the fabric. Close up you see dimension and details that make the difference, including double welt trim and fabric-covered faceplate. Design: Glenna Cook Interiors. Upholstered walls: Anthony Vella.

PAINT
Minimum Expense, Maximum Appeal

Line That Defines
Bold touch of color on moldings focuses attention on walls and openings, drawing outdoor greenery into a cheerful room that encourages long visits. Design: Nancy Bostwick.

Bold Color Slant

Yellow walls and contrasting white ceiling and cubbyhole accentuate diagonal lines of bedroom. Use of child's favorite color turns difficult space into a special hideaway. Design: Marcia Armstrong.

Subtle Artistry

Colors combine successfully when used at the same intensity. Apricot ceiling and pink and beige walls, accented by blue bedspread, work together for a serene setting that only looks expensive. Design: Osburn Design.

. . . PAINT

Pick of the Palette

Color Mastery
Sophisticated shades of one color on cabinets, walls, and ceiling create a contemporary look that delights even the most critical eye. Concealed lighting is directed at the ceiling for distinctive effect. Design: Osburn Design.

Accent on Color

Complementary colors of the same intensity are great companions. Here, orange and blue with accents of white create an eye-appealing dining room and kitchen that flow into one. Design: Olga Rackovich.

Color between the Lines

Striking use of color inside a framework of detailed molding gives prominence to architectural lines, displays cherished possessions to special advantage. Design: Lois Lugonja.

Mixed to Match

Graceful antique scroll was the starting point for this design scheme. Mixing paint for color match was the next step, followed by careful selection of furnishings, carpet, and accessories. Design: Julie S. Haas.

. . . PAINT
Pattern Panache

Treasured Heirloom
Imitating the handmade patchwork quilt on the bed, the stencil pattern on the wall above acts as headboard and becomes masterpiece in its own right. Design: Robert W. Vinson.

Creative Embellishment
Lilies bloom the year around in this clean, crisp wall treatment. Bathroom's existing wallpaper needed zest, and bright stenciling did the trick. Design: Phyllis Dunstan.

Americana
Ceiling-level floral border meanders around the walls, adding a sparkle of color. Stencil design echoes the colors of antique quilts abounding in the bedroom. Design: Delsa Ham. Stenciling: Liddy Schmidt and Linda Kilgore.

Springtime Bouquets
In upbeat version of an old art form, stenciled flowers, inspired by a quilt for a child's bed, dance across the walls. Rows of dots on the walls and flower arrangements near the ceiling line unify the whimsical design. Design: Julie S. Haas. Stenciling: Liddy Schmidt and Linda Kilgore.

Country Classic
Traditional stencil designs of borders and single medallions reappear in an updated country kitchen. Subtle shades of color applied over the specially textured walls reinforce the antique appearance. Design: Liddy Schmidt and Linda Kilgore.

... PAINT
Special Effects

Mural in a Kit

Expanding baby's horizons is a colorful rainbow design that came from a paint kit. If you're unsure about your creative talents but want a wall full of color, a kit can be just the answer. Choose a design and follow the manufacturer's color suggestions, or pick your own colors. Instructions lead you through every step, from bare walls to fantasy-filled rooms.

Visual Deception

Notice anything unusual about this kitchen corner? Look again at the paneling, Dutch door, trinket-filled shelves, and outdoor panorama. None are real; they're all products of an artist's brush. Only the door handle, dried leaves, and bird cage pass three-dimensional inspection on these walls. In a style called *tromp l'oeil* (literally, "fool the eye"), the mural opens up a tight, dark corner. Careful shading creates the illusion of reality. Mural: Asche LaBash Studios.

Whimsical Walls
Playful animals parade along a flower-lined pathway in this fanciful painted scene. The mural fills walls with soft color—and learning experiences. Mural: Sidney MacDonald Russell.

Linear Wizardry
Strategically placed lines of color focus attention on the bed, then carry the eye up, over, and around a youngster's room. Easy and inexpensive, design has ageless appeal that will last for years. Design: Phyllis Dunstan.

Taming a Tall Wall
Big, bold graphic controls room size and provides easy transition for the eye between upper and lower levels. The design moves uninterrupted across custom-made blinds. To ensure proper alignment, the blinds were hung before the wall was painted. Design: Carol A. Tanzi.

PANELING
The Many Faces of Pine

Understated Elegance
Vertical pine boards left in their natural state add handsome, timeless beauty to a dining room. Heirloom quilt and contemporary art and furnishings are equally at home.

Country Charm
Warmth and hospitality flow from a cozy kitchen paneled with horizontal knotty pine boards. The fabric on the windows and bench complements the yellow cast of the wood in this cheery breakfast nook. Design: Carol A. Tanzi.

Handsome Results from Humble Beginnings

Strips of pine lath cover upper half of bathroom walls in warm, natural tones. Thinner and less expensive than regular board paneling, lath strips can be installed quickly with adhesive or brad nails. Design: Joseph Price.

Contemporary Signature

White stain on pine boards produces a clean, modern look. Ceiling paneling flows horizontally down one wall, vertically down the adjacent wall for dramatic effect.

...PANELING

The Lines of Wood

Pattern and Texture in Tandem

Weathered fir boards in herringbone pattern make a spectacular wall treatment; oak trim outlines the design. Rich texture and color of paneling offset the brick wall's ruggedness. Design: The Grapevine Woodworks/Greg Dean, Designer.

Majestic Environs

Walnut sheet paneling soars to great heights, standing up to the grandeur of the outdoors. To span height, 4 by 8 sheets were butted, and seams were covered with molding. Careful planning enabled the owners to match panel grooves so well that sheets appear to continue past the molding without a break.

Noble Lines

Painting wood wainscoting and ceiling molding to match walls expands and brightens a room. Now more dramatic, detailed moldings add classic beauty.

Natural Beauty
Natural oak boards in random lengths provide a timeless bedroom backdrop. Paneling's grain patterns and clean vertical lines blend perfectly with fabric on furnishings. Architect: Michael Moyer.

Distinctive Design
Installed over old wall covering in a major face lift, resawn cedar board paneling unifies a family room's furnishings. Paneling's clean lines and warm tones keep the room open and inviting. Matching wood shelving is functional, yet preserves spacious feeling of the room. Architect: James Bryant.

WALLPAPER
THE OPTIONS ARE ENDLESS

Today there's a lot more than paper behind the use of the word "wallpaper." Many other materials—including vinyls, metallics, grasscloths, fibers, fabrics, and wood veneers—are lending new life to old walls. The home decorating industry has even adopted a new terminology for all these types of rolled materials—they're called "wallcoverings."

As you shop for wallpaper, you''ll soon discover that choosing one is not as easy as you first imagined. The myriad options in materials, styles, colors, and patterns, as well as coordinating borders and fabrics, will have you dizzy from all the creative applications you'll be visualizing. You'll also find many wallpapers that are prepasted, scrubbable, and strippable, features that make application, cleaning, and removal a snap.

To help you make your decision, we begin this chapter with a description of the types of wallpapers available, as well as instructions for determining how much you'll need to order.

Regardless of the kind of wallpaper you choose, taking time for adequate surface preparation is very important. Information on how to prepare your walls begins on page 38. Detailed directions for cutting and hanging the wallpaper follow. Hints are included to make these steps easier than you ever imagined.

YOUR CHOICES IN MATERIALS

When you're ready to begin shopping for wallpaper, be prepared to spend many hours looking through the hundreds of samples in the manufacturers' books. Often, the books will have color photographs of rooms decorated with those wallpapers, allowing you to see how a pattern looks when it's repeated across a whole wall, and how the pattern's size relates to the rest of the room.

The sample book will also provide information on the size of a pattern repeat, the yardage in a bolt, the type of adhesive to use, the care instructions, and the cost. Take all of these into consideration in making your final decision.

If you're a beginner, you may want to consider prepasted and pre-trimmed wallpapers (see page 35). Also, take into account the function of the room to determine if you need a scrubbable wallpaper or if a washable finish is sufficient (see page 35).

Most shops let you borrow their sample books overnight. Take this opportunity to see how a particular wallpaper will work in your home. Note how it looks in the light of the room, how it blends with the existing colors, and most importantly, how

roper Equipment—and Patience
hese are the building blocks of a suc-
essful wallpapering project. With just a
w essential tools, you can transform
ooms with ordinary walls into attractive,
ersonalized living spaces.

you and your family react to having it there.

It may be that you'll spend days thumbing through samples and carrying books back and forth to the store. But once you've decided on material and pattern, the actual hanging may take only a weekend.

STANDARD WALLPAPER

Standard wallpapers are normally printed either on a machine roller or by a hand-printed silk-screen process. Both methods can create patterns with subtle shading and a feeling of depth.

Machine-printed papers are inexpensive because they're produced by a high-speed, large-volume process. They're generally pretrimmed (see page 35).

Silk-screened papers, on the other hand, are artistic, individual, and costly. Because of the hand processes involved, certain irregularities in pattern are unavoidable. Usually, silk-screened papers have selvages (see page 35) that need to be trimmed before the paper is hung.

When selecting a standard wallpaper, note that the cheapest paper isn't always the best buy. Because it's generally pulpy and porous, inexpensive wallpaper absorbs moisture readily and can tear easily during installation.

VINYL

Vinyl wall coverings range from those sprayed with a thin coating of vinyl to solid vinyls backed with paper or fabric.

Vinyl coatings give wall coverings a washable surface, but wall coverings treated this way aren't particularly durable or grease-resistant.

Solid vinyls are hard-wearing, scrubbable, and stain-resistant. They're available in a wide variety of colors and textures, some of which imitate grasscloth, wood, or silk. Use solid vinyls where hard-

working walls are a must—in children's bedrooms, dens, bathrooms, and kitchens.

For tips on installing vinyl, see page 50.

FOIL

Foil wallpaper is made from a very thin, flexible metallic sheet—either aluminum or simulated metal—laminated to a paper or fabric backing. Some foils are coated with mylar; these have a highly reflective mirror finish and are scrubbable.

Foils are printed in many colors. Some are mottled to resemble marble or tortoise shell, a gilt-etched mirror, or other light-reflecting surfaces. Others have bold patterns.

The reflective qualities of foil wall coverings make them good candidates for rooms that need to be brightened or opened up. Keep in mind, though, that foils are hard to hang because they wrinkle easily. Once on the wall, they'll show any imperfection on the wall's surface; usually, you'll need to use lining paper (see page 35) under the foil. See page 50 for more information on applying foil.

ORIENTAL WEAVES & NATURAL TEXTURES

Coverings of weaves, such as grasscloth and other fibers, and natural materials like cork can add beauty and richness to your walls. Installing these wall coverings requires some special care; see page 50 for installation pointers.

Oriental weaves: grasscloth, burlap, hemp & other fibers

The three most popular oriental weaves—grasscloth, burlap, and hemp—are widely used in home decorating. A fourth group of yarn and jute is a new addition to this field and is quickly gaining popularity. All of these weaves are available laminated on paper backing.

A roll of woven material can range in price from moderate to very costly, depending on the origin of the material and the type of weave.

Though many oriental weaves have no particular pattern, some are manufactured with patterns such as basket weave and herringbone. Some even have a decorative pattern printed on the face of the texture. The color uniformity of all oriental weaves varies slightly.

Grasscloth. Depending on the texture, color, and type of weave, grasscloth can look oriental, tropical, casual, or highly sophisticated. This versatility makes it very popular today.

Real grasscloth is made from arrowroot bark imported from Japan. Because of the shortage of this bark, though, synthetic materials are often substituted for real grasscloth.

Since grasscloth has no pattern, installing it involves no matching. As with most weaves, it's natural for the seams to show.

Hemp. Though it resembles grasscloth, hemp has a much finer weave. Still, it contains all the natural irregularities and color variations of grasscloth, and the seams will be prominent.

Burlap. It's been a long upward climb for burlap since the days when it served chiefly as sacking for rice. Now you can buy natural or colored burlap in bolts and cut it into strips to cover your wall. Burlap on which patterns have been silk-screened is also available in many colors.

Since the color uniformity of burlap doesn't vary as much as that of grasscloth or hemp, seams are less noticeable. It's an ideal surface on which to hang pictures or notes because it's durable and doesn't show tack marks.

Yarn and jute. To make wall coverings from these natural fibers, machine or hand-spun yarn or jute is laminated to a paper backing. Available in shades of wheat, brown, or gray, fiber wall coverings are valued for their sound-absorbing quality and their interesting textures. Generally, they're quite costly.

The fiber strands are usually strung vertically on the paper, but some are woven in a basket weave or other pattern. Because of intrinsic shade variations, matching isn't possible and seams may show.

Natural textures: cork & wood veneers

You can get exciting results from covering your walls with cork or a wood veneer. But since both materials are costly and can be difficult to install, you may want to consider having a professional do the job for you.

Cork. The natural shading properties of cork add to the beauty of this material. Good for muffling sound, cork is also functional—it's a perfect wall-size tack board.

(Continued on next page)

WALLPAPERING TERMS YOU SHOULD KNOW

Bolt. Two or more continuous rolls of wallpaper in a single package.

Booking. Folding the cut ends of a freshly pasted wallpaper strip, pasted sides together, so ends butt and side edges are exactly aligned. This allows the paste to penetrate the strip thoroughly without saturating it and keeps it moist until ready to hang. Booking also prevents shrinkage; a porous wallpaper will do all its shrinking in this stage, rather than on the wall.

Companion fabric. Fabric printed in the same pattern as that on a wallpaper. Because of differences in materials, dyes, and printing processes, the color values in companion fabrics are rarely identical to those in the wallpaper.

Companion or coordinated wallpapers. A set of two or more wallpapers designed or colored to coordinate with one another.

Lining paper. Inexpensive blank paper stock recommended for smoothing wall surfaces and absorbing excess moisture. Originally designed to act as a breathable layer between a foil wall covering and the wall, lining paper is now available in several weights, the heaviest weight being sturdy enough to provide a smooth working surface over brick and cinder block walls.

Pattern repeat. The vertical distance between a point on a pattern and the next point where the pattern is identical.

Peelable wallpaper. Wallpaper that can be removed from a wall by peeling off the top layer. Only a thin residue of paper is left on the wall. The residue is easily removed with a sponge and warm water.

Prepasted wallpaper. Wallpaper that has been coated at the factory with a water-soluble adhesive. Instead of applying adhesive to it before hanging, you simply soak it in water.

Pretrimmed wallpaper. Wallpaper from which the selvage has been trimmed at the factory.

Run number. The number given to a separate printing of a pattern. Since printings may vary in color and intensity, always specify the desired run number as well as the pattern number if you have to order additional wallpaper.

Scrubbable wall covering. Wall covering that's durable enough to be scrubbed with a soft brush and a mild soap.

Selvage. The unprinted side edge of a wallpaper that protects it and sometimes carries instructions for its use. The selvage must be trimmed before the wallpaper is hung.

Size (also sizing). A liquid coating applied to wall surfaces that seals the surface, helps the adhesive grip the wall, and allows the installer to move the wallpaper into position more easily. You can buy commercially prepared size or make your own from wallpaper paste diluted to half strength.

Strip. A length of wallpaper cut to fit the height of a wall. In murals, a single section of the design.

Strippable wallpaper. Wallpaper that can be removed from a wall by hand without tearing or leaving any film or paper residue.

Washable wallpaper. Wallpaper that can be cleaned with mild soap and water without being damaged. Washability varies with different wallpapers—soil, grease, and stains may not always be removable from such wallpapers.

Paper-backed cork comes in a variety of thicknesses, weights, and colors. Among the patterns available are diamond, parquet, and stripe.

Specialty wood veneers. If you're fond of natural wood grain but don't want to install board or sheet paneling, consider a paper or cloth-backed covering made from wood veneer.

These flexible wall coverings, available in a variety of woods, effectively display the natural wood grain. Each strip is longer than wood sheet paneling, but not as wide. Because of the way the wood is sliced from the tree, you can match grain lines from strip to strip. Wood veneer wall covering must be custom ordered.

FLOCKED WALLPAPER

Two-dimensional flocked wallpaper is produced by a machine that shakes finely chopped nylon or rayon fibers over paper on which a pattern has just been printed with slow-drying paint. The texture of the finished paper resembles that of damask or cut velvet.

Flocked wallpaper isn't suitable for a casual room, since this material has a definite air of elegance. It adds texture and visual warmth to a room and successfully hides imperfections on the walls.

You can find flocked paper in many colors and patterns. Avoid using it in areas that collect dirt or receive a lot of wear. Special installation instructions are on page 50.

MURALS & SPECIAL MOUNTINGS

Murals are hand-screened, machine-printed, or lithographed pictorial designs pieced together in several strips of wallpaper. Special mountings can take the form of a blown-up Picasso painting or even a family photograph enlarged many times to fit wall-size dimensions.

Both types are illusion-makers, drawing the eye into their depths and seemingly enlarging the room. They range in price from the relatively inexpensive ready-made photo murals to the very costly designer scenic murals.

Murals to expand your horizons

Photo murals—photos enlarged to room size—usually depict a natural setting, such as farm lands, a seascape, or a view from a mountain top. You can piece strips to create a scene that covers an entire wall, or hang them individually for a little less drama.

Murals can also portray a historical setting or symbolic depiction of an event or era. Look for murals in wallpaper stores or in interior design studios. Often, you can find solid color wallpaper of the same material to cover the remaining wall area.

Murals are printed on a variety of materials; follow any special instructions that apply to the one you're using.

Special mountings—the show stoppers

Because they're custom-made, enlargements of actual scenes or paintings can be among the most expensive of all wallpaper. Color enlargements cost three times as much as black and white.

You can have a special mounting made at a studio specializing in general graphics (look under "Photo Copying" in the Yellow Pages). The studio can work from 4 by 5 negatives, positive prints, 35mm slides, material from books or magazines, or original graphic materials. When you order the print, be sure it will fit the area you want to cover.

In processing color mountings, the dealer must intensify color in the reproduction because the increase in photo size reduces the density of the negative's color.

The enlargement can be silk-screened on a variety of materials, including paper, vinyl, linen, mylar, jute, burlap, grasscloth, and cork. Check with your wallpaper dealer about the best way to hang the mounting.

FABRIC-LAMINATED WALLPAPERS

Fabrics are a unique way to add interest to walls. Most fabrics, except those that have naps or are loosely woven, can be laminated to paper for hanging. Inquire about this service at an interior design shop or a wallpaper store. The various techniques for applying fabric *directly* to the walls are described on pages 53–63.

If you want to cover your walls with the same pattern as your bedding, draperies, or upholstery, using the actual fabric for the walls will give you an exact match. Many times, printed wallpapers made to coordinate with companion fabrics don't match well because the dyes used in the wallpaper are slightly different than those used for the fabric.

Decorator fabrics are the best choice for these laminated coverings because the patterns are usually printed so an adjoining strip of fabric picks up the vertical pattern design where the first strip left off. Once the selvages are trimmed, the strips can be butted together with no overlapping.

For special installation instructions, see page 51.

CARPETING

Both lightweight standard and indoor-outdoor carpeting are occasionally used as a wall covering. When installed on a wall, carpeting requires little maintenance, shows no scrapes or scratches, and reduces noise considerably.

Carpets come in a wide choice of patterns and textures, and span a broad price range. Dealers can recommend specific techniques for attaching carpeting to walls.

PLAN BEFORE YOU BUY

It pays to make a generous estimate of your needs when purchasing wallpaper. If you run short during installation and need to order additional rolls, you may not be able to obtain an exact color match. And if you need to patch damaged areas later, you'll be glad to have matching material on hand.

During each printing, manufacturers use fresh batches of colored ink. Each newly mixed batch of color is identified by a run number printed on the package of each bolt of wallpaper. Check that all your bolts have the same number before you even unroll them.

Choosing the proper adhesive (see page 38) is equally important. Be sure to use the adhesive recommended for the type of covering you're installing.

FIGURING YOUR WALLPAPER NEEDS

To decide how much wallpaper you need, first measure the wall or room with a steel tape. Use a notebook to record your figures. You'll want to take the notebook with you later when you're shopping for your wallpaper; this way, you can be sure to purchase the amount you need.

Measure the height and width of each wall (including openings); then multiply the two figures to determine the total area of the wall in square feet. Add the square footage of all the walls to be covered to determine the total area.

After you figure a room's total square footage including openings, deduct 15 square feet for every average-size door or window. For larger or unusually shaped openings, measure the height and width of each opening and deduct the exact square footage from your total.

How many rolls?

Once you've calculated and recorded the total square footage of wall space to be covered (with openings deducted), you'll need to determine the number of single rolls of wallpaper needed. Though you can estimate the amount using the chart below, the following instructions will give you a more accurate count.

Though priced by the single roll, wall covering is sold in multiple-roll bolts. Coverings vary in width from 21 to 36 inches, but they have the same total square footage, depending on whether they're standard or European rolls. This means that wider rolls are shorter in length than narrower rolls.

A standard single roll contains 36 square feet of material. The cutting and trimming you'll do will deduct about 6 square feet, so figure on 30 square feet of usable wallpaper from each roll you buy.

A European single roll contains 29 square feet. After cutting and trimming, plan on having 25 square feet of usable material per roll.

To figure the total number of single rolls you need, divide the total square footage of wall space by 30 (25 for European rolls) square feet. If you're left with a fractional remainder of square feet, buy an additional roll.

Allow for pattern repeats

If you're using patterned wallpaper, you can't accurately estimate the number of rolls you need until you figure out the number of pattern re-

---

ESTIMATING WALLPAPER

For a quick and generally reliable estimate of the number of rolls of wallpaper you'll need to cover your room, use the chart below. This type of chart is found in the front of most sample books.

Distance Around Room in Feet	Number of Single Rolls Needed			Number of Yards for Borders	Single Rolls for Ceiling
	Height of Ceiling				
	8 Feet	9 Feet	10 Feet		
28	8	8	10	11	2
30	8	8	10	11	2
32	8	10	10	12	2
34	10	10	12	13	4
36	10	10	12	13	4
38	10	12	12	14	4
40	10	12	12	15	4
42	12	12	14	15	4
44	12	12	14	16	4
46	12	14	14	17	6
48	14	14	16	17	6
50	14	14	16	18	6
52	14	14	16	19	6
54	14	16	18	19	6
56	14	16	18	20	8
58	16	16	18	21	8
60	16	18	20	21	8
62	16	18	20	22	8

peats that will fit your actual wall height. Pattern books provide the repeat height on the back of each pattern page. Note that a drop match pattern (see "Straight match or drop match?" on page 43) requires only half the number of inches as its repeat measurement.

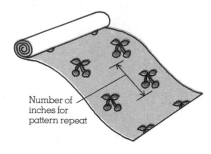

Number of inches for pattern repeat

To allow for pattern repeat, divide the height (in inches) of the wall by the number of inches between the pattern repeat; if you have a fractional remainder, round it off to the next highest number. For example, a 96-inch wall height divided by an 18-inch pattern repeat gives you 5.33 repeats, rounded off to 6.

Then, multiply the repeat measurement by the number of repeats you'll need to determine the working height figure you must use. In the case above, multiplying the 18-inch pattern repeat by 6 repeats tells you that you must calculate your wallpaper needs according to the requirements of the 108-inch wall, rather than the actual 96-inch wall.

If, as in this case, the actual wall height differs from the height required by your pattern repeat, purchase the additional number of rolls necessary to allow for your pattern repeats.

Borders

You may want to hang a coordinating border around the room at the top of the walls. To determine the amount of border, measure the width (in feet) of all walls to be covered and divide by three. Since borders are sold by the yard, this will give you the number of yards needed.

If you plan to use the border in any other areas, measure them and

add to the yardage accordingly. Include some additional working length for mitering the corners around openings, if necessary.

CHOOSING THE PROPER ADHESIVE

Wallpaper dealers stock adhesives for every type of installation. To find an adhesive suitable for your material, check the manufacturer's instructions, or ask your dealer.

Adhesives come in both dry and premixed forms. Dry adhesive is made from a wheat formula; premixed is made from a nonorganic or synthetic formula.

You can use either dry adhesive or the premixed adhesive recommended by the wallpaper manufacturer to apply porous materials such as standard papers and oriental weaves. If you're planning to add a protective coating (see page 52) to a porous wall covering, always use premixed vinyl adhesive, rather than dry adhesive, to prevent mildew.

To install nonporous coverings—vinyls, foils, mylars, and other specially treated materials—use premixed adhesive; its low moisture content makes it mildew-resistant.

PREPARING THE SURFACE

Before hanging wallpaper, you must make sure that walls are completely clean and totally free from damage. Preparation required for any wall includes removing lighting fixtures and faceplates, as well as cleaning and rinsing the wall thoroughly.

Depending on the condition of the wall, you may also have to strip the old wallpaper (if there is one), repair all cracks and holes, and apply an undercoat. An undercoat,

or primer, is especially important when hanging strippable wallpaper; if the wall isn't properly prepared, the wallpaper won't be removable.

How you clean and prepare your wall depends on the type of wall, its condition, and the kind of covering you're installing.

PREPARING AN ALREADY PAPERED WALL

If your existing wallpaper is in good condition, only one layer, and not textured, you can probably hang wallpaper over it after a few preparatory steps. But if you plan to hang a nonporous covering, most manufacturers recommend that you completely remove any old wallpaper.

Leaving old wallpaper on the wall. Once you've established that the covering already on the wall is basically in good condition, check it for air bubbles (puncture them) or loose corners or seams. Glue them down with the same adhesive you'll use to install the new covering.

Carefully check old seams; if necessary, sand and fill them with spackling compound (see page 70). Fill all cracks and holes with spackle or patching plaster and sand when dry. Apply a coat of flat, oil-base enamel undercoat to the wall; allow it to dry for 24 hours. (Without this undercoat, the paste may not adhere properly and strippable coverings won't be strippable.)

Check the instructions that
(Continued on page 40)

Helpful Wallpapering Tools

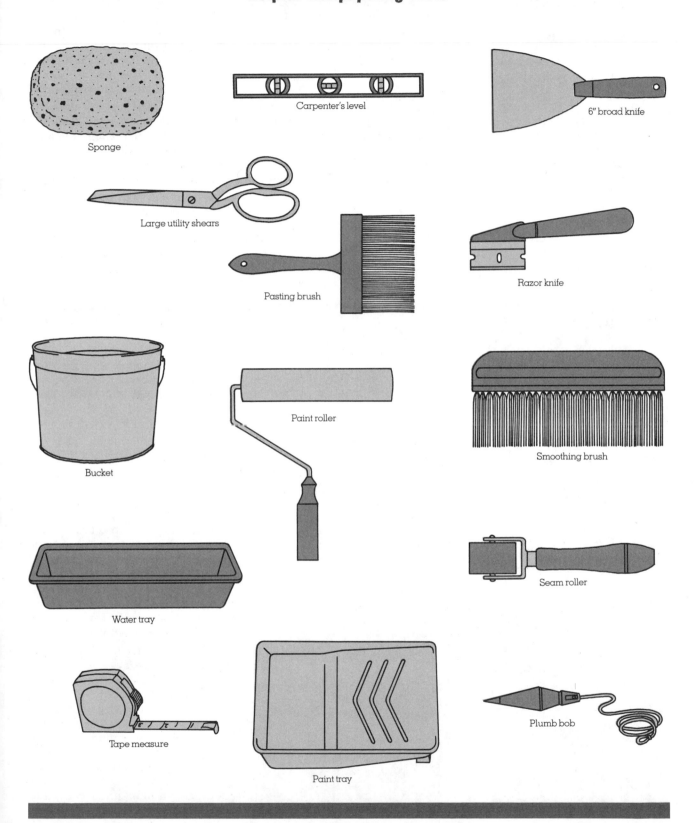

Sponge

Carpenter's level

6" broad knife

Large utility shears

Pasting brush

Razor knife

Bucket

Paint roller

Smoothing brush

Water tray

Seam roller

Tape measure

Paint tray

Plumb bob

come with the wallpaper to find out if you need to size the wall (see page 35) before hanging the covering.

If the existing wallpaper is a foil or a specially treated, nonstrippable material, or if your wall is covered with cloth-backed vinyl hung over gypsum board without a sealer, then you must apply a special vinyl-to-vinyl primer to the wall before hanging the new material. This will ensure proper drying of the adhesive and prevent mildew.

Removing old wallpaper. Wallpaper in poor condition, multiple layers of wallpaper, and flocked wallpaper must be removed before you can hang a new covering. If the existing material is strippable, it will come off easily when you pull it up at a corner or seam.

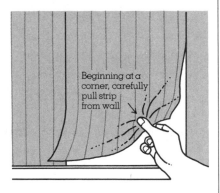

Beginning at a corner, carefully pull strip from wall

Before removing a nonstrippable wallpaper, break the surface of the covering by sanding it with very coarse sandpaper or by scoring the wall with a saw (scrape the saw's entire cutting blade against the covering in many places and in any direction).

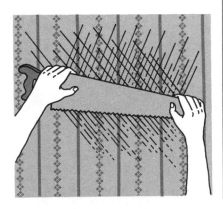

To remove the wallpaper, you can use either a steamer, available for rent from your dealer, or a garden sprayer. Sometimes, you can add a liquid to the water to hasten the paste-dissolving process, but ask your dealer before adding anything to the water.

A steamer converts water to steam that runs through a hose to a pan with a trigger. You simply move the pan slowly along the wall, allowing steam to penetrate the covering. To use a garden sprayer, you just fill it with very hot water and spray the water onto the wallpaper.

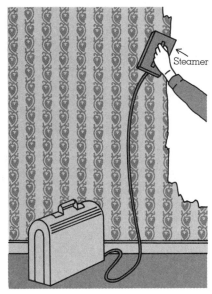

Steamer

In a matter of minutes, you can begin to remove the old material. Using a broad knife and working down from the top of the wall,

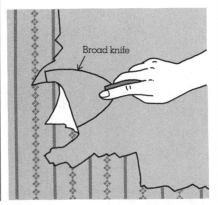

Broad knife

scrape off the wallpaper. If it doesn't pull away easily, dampen it again; don't force it with the knife. Work carefully to avoid nicking or chipping the wall's surface.

In cases where the wall has been covered with several layers of wallpaper, you'll find it easier to remove one layer at a time. If a nonporous sealer was used on any one of these layers, first sand it or score it in many places with a saw blade. After applying steam or water, allow time for the wallpaper to loosen; then peel it off. (Since nonporous sealers are not water soluble, you must get the water behind the wallpaper before it can effectively loosen the paste.)

If you find that the original layer was applied directly to the wall and cannot be removed without damaging the wall, stop at that layer. Allow the wall to dry thoroughly (wait at least 12 hours). Spackle any nicks you may have made in removing previous layers of wallpaper; then sand the wall smooth and seal again. Finally, apply a coat of flat, oil-base enamel undercoat and hang the new material.

Wall coverings pasted directly to gypsum board without an undercoat of a nonporous sealer will be almost impossible to remove without damaging the board. Seal the wall with a coat of flat, oil-base enamel undercoat.

PREPARING A NEWLY PLASTERED WALL

A freshly plastered wall must be thoroughly dry (the type of plaster used will dictate the drying time—ask your builder) before it can be covered. When the wall is completely cured, seal it with a coat of 2-pound cut shellac or flat, oil-base primer-sealer; allow it to dry. Size, if necessary (see page 35), and hang the wallpaper.

PREPARING A NEW GYPSUM BOARD WALL

Before papering over a new gypsum board wall, tape and spackle all joints between panels with taping compound. When dry, sand the wall smooth and apply a coat of flat, oil-base primer-sealer. When the primer is dry, size the wall, if necessary (see page 35).

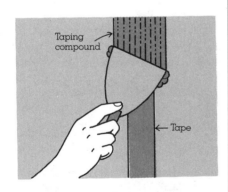

Taping compound

Tape

PREPARING A PAINTED WALL

Wallpaper is often applied to plaster or gypsum board surfaces that have been previously painted. If your old painted wall is in good condition, simply clean off all dirt, grease, and

oil, and let it dry. (To repair holes and other surface damage, see page 70.)

If the existing paint is a flat, oil-base one, size, if necessary (see page 35), and hang the wallpaper. But if it's latex paint, or if you don't know what type of paint was used, you must apply a coat of flat, oil-base undercoat.

PREPARING A WOOD WALL

To be successfully covered, a wood wall must be flat and smooth. For directions on preparing a textured wall, see the instructions below. Tape and fill all joints and cracks with taping compound. If the wood has a wax finish on it, remove all wax. Then sand the surface and apply a coat of flat, oil base enamel undercoat.

PREPARING A TEXTURED WALL

The textured surfaces of some gypsum board and plaster walls and the rough finishes of some wood walls must be made smooth before you can cover them. The most efficient way to do this is to coat the wall with a gypsum taping compound and sand it after the compound dries. Then apply a coat of flat, oil-base primer-sealer and let it dry thoroughly (about 24 hours).

Hanging a heavyweight lining paper (see page 35) over a textured wall, even one as rough as brick or cinder block, will also smooth the surface.

PREPARING A CONCRETE OR CEMENT-PRODUCT WALL

Concrete walls are found in some modern condominiums and highrise buildings. Before any wallpaper can be applied to these walls, you must remove all dirt and grease (see page 70 for a recommended cleaner). When walls are clean and thoroughly dry, apply a coat of flat, oil-base pigmented sealer. When this has dried completely, follow

with a coat of flat, oil-base enamel undercoat.

Sometimes, a cement wall will be so roughly textured that furring (see page 88) and adding gypsum board or plastering over it may seem to be the only way to make it flat enough for wallpaper. An alternative is to apply heavyweight lining paper (see page 35). The heaviest weight lining paper available is thick and stiff, making it somewhat difficult to handle (you may want to wear work gloves), but it can turn a cement wall into a surface smooth enough for wallpaper.

Below-grade concrete walls, such as those found in basements and in lower levels of many split-level homes, should be furred (see page 88) and covered with gypsum board. This will provide a smooth and sound foundation for wallpaper, as well as help to insulate the room.

PREPARING A MILDEWED WALL

Mildew is primarily caused by a fungus living on damp, organic material. These spores cause staining of walls and other surfaces. Before you can paper a mildewed wall, you must remove all existing fungal spores (and any wallpaper, see page 40). One effective method is to scrub all affected areas with the following solution:

⅔ cup trisodium phosphate
⅓ cup strong detergent
1 quart bleach
3 quarts warm water

Another method is to use a concentrated liquid mildew eradicator that can be purchased from your paint dealer. Wearing gloves and protecting your eyes, apply either solution with a brush, scrubbing vigorously. Allow the solution to remain on the surface for a few minutes and then rinse well.

Let the surface dry for 2 days. Then apply a coat of flat, oil-base enamel undercoat into which you have mixed a commercially available fungicide additive. Let the walls dry.

HANGING THE WALLPAPER

The following pages take you through the basic steps for hanging standard wallpaper. It's wise to read through these steps before you begin cutting and pasting. Also note the exceptions to the rules in the section "Different Wallpapers—Different Installations" on page 50.

If you're planning to cover the ceiling as well as the walls, you must complete the ceiling before you begin the walls. See "How to Handle a Ceiling" on page 51 for directions. Apply borders last of all (see page 52).

For special instructions or advice, consult your dealer. Some dealers even conduct lectures or show films on hanging wallpaper.

EQUIPMENT & SUPPLIES

Before starting any wallpaper project, make sure you have all the necessary equipment and supplies on hand. You may be able to rent some equipment from your dealer.

Use large plastic **drop cloths** to cover furniture, floors, and rugs in both the area being covered and the area around the pasting table. (Consider pasting and booking strips of wallpaper in the garage or a workroom.)

You'll need a table large enough to hold your wallpaper strips. Use a sturdy **work table** or cover a table with a large sheet of plywood. Put your **stepladder** into place near the wall and clear a path between the pasting table and the foot of the ladder.

Essential tools include large **utility shears** and a **razor knife** with **utility razor blades** for cutting and trimming wallpaper; you'll also need a **broad knife, seam roller, smoothing brush** (or squeegee for vinyl coverings), **sponge,** and flexible **steel tape measure.**

A **metal straightedge** (up to 6 feet long) is helpful as a guide for cutting the selvages of untrimmed wallpaper. A **carpenter's level** or a **plumb bob** is necessary to establish the true vertical line of the walls.

For *unpasted wallpaper*, you'll need a sufficient amount of the recommended **adhesive** (see the manufacturer's instructions) and a **paint tray, bucket,** and wide, soft **paint roller** or **pasting brush** for applying it.

For *prepasted wallpaper*, only a long, narrow **water tray** is needed.

WHERE TO BEGIN

You'll need to give some thought to where on a wall is the best place to hang your first strip. Because the last strip you hang probably won't match the first, plan to finish in the least conspicuous place. Usually—if your room has no special openings such as a fireplace or picture window—the best place to begin is at a corner, a door casing, or a window casing on the wall that's least noticeable. You'll move around the room to the point where you began.

If you find you have some common (and often puzzling) wall situations, here are some suggestions on where to start.

Wall with two windows. When papering a wall with two windows, locate the first strip between the two windows, not at the wall's corner. You can do this either by positioning the edge of the strip between the two windows, or by locating the center line of the strip between the two windows.

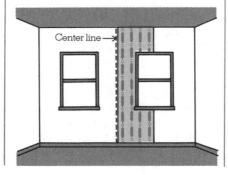

Work from the center out to both corners of the wall. Continue hanging wallpaper from one corner around the room to the other corner.

Wall with a fireplace or picture window. On a wall with a fireplace or picture window, hang the first strip above the fireplace or window. Do this either by positioning the edge of the strip at the center of the fireplace or picture window, or by positioning the strip's center line at the center of the fireplace or window. Continue around the room as described above.

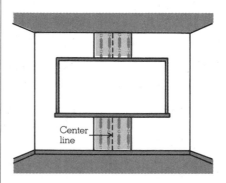

ESTABLISHING PLUMB

Most house walls are not straight and plumb (perfectly vertical). So when you're papering, you'll want to establish a plumb line, instead of aligning the strip with a corner that is perhaps imperfectly vertical.

First, locate where to put the line: figure the width of your wallpaper minus ½ inch; measure this distance from a corner, window, door, or some other starting point, and mark the wall there.

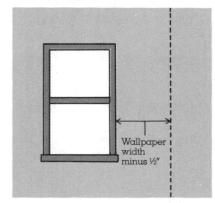

Now you're ready to establish plumb. You can do it in either of two ways:

1) Hold a carpenter's level flat against the wall, vertically aligning one edge with the mark. Adjust the level until the bubble that designates plumb is centered. Draw a line along the level's edge, straight down from your mark. Continue this process, connecting lines until you have a floor-to-ceiling plumb line.

2) You can also establish plumb using a plumb bob or a weight at the end of a string on which you've rubbed soft chalk. Locate where to put the line as described above, making the mark on the wall at the ceiling line. Place a tack in the wall at the mark and tie the string's end to the tack so the plumb bob's point (or the weight's point) dangles a fraction of an inch above the baseboard. Once it stops swinging back and forth, press the lower end of the string against the wall and snap the line.

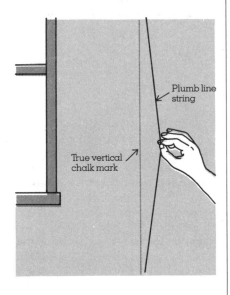

Plumb line string

True vertical chalk mark

INSPECTING, MATCHING PATTERNS, CUTTING & PASTING

Before you take the irrevocable step of cutting strips of wallpaper, it's important to examine the material for any defects; you'll also want to decide how you'll cut and paste it. Be aware, also, of any special instructions that apply to the type of wallpaper you're hanging (see page 50).

Make an inspection & take inventory

Most wall coverings come with specific directions from the manufacturer. Read them all the way through before you open the first package.

Before measuring and cutting the wallpaper, examine each bolt and check that the run numbers (see page 35) match. Also make sure there are no flaws in printing or variations in shading.

The next step is to take the vertical curl out of the wallpaper. Pull out 3 to 4 feet of the roll at a time and draw this length firmly over the edge of a table, face side up. Then reroll the covering so it curls the opposite way from the way it was packaged.

If you find any defects in the material, immediately return it to the store for replacement. No manufacturer or retailer will accept responsibility for defects after the product is on the wall. If you delay, you may not find your pattern, texture, or color in the same run number.

Straight match or drop match?

The two basic kinds of patterns are straight match and drop match. With a straight match pattern, the design along the top edge of a strip of wallpaper starts and ends at the same vertical point in the pattern. When the pattern of a second strip is aligned with the first, the design along the top edge of the second strip is the same as the design along the top edge of the first strip.

With a drop match pattern, the pattern at one side edge of a strip is half a repeat lower than the other edge. The second strip must be "dropped" until the pattern repeats are aligned. The designs along the top edge are the same on every other strip.

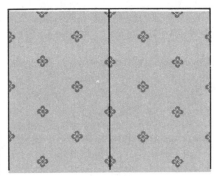

Drop match

Before you cut, study the pattern to determine how you want it to appear on the wall. After you decide which pattern match your design has, you're ready to measure and cut the strips.

Cutting the wallpaper

Because ceiling heights can vary, it's a good idea to measure the wall height before cutting each strip of

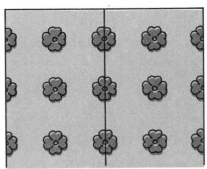

Straight match

SHOP TALK

When cutting and trimming wall strips, you'll get the cleanest cut by resigning yourself to the fact that razor blades are short-lived.

For most materials, you should change the blade after two or three cuts. But for the cleanest cut with grasscloth and other oriental weaves, change the blade for each strip.

wallpaper. Transfer this measurement to the wallpaper, leaving 2 inches extra at the top and bottom. Be sure to allow for pattern match on each strip, if necessary.

Using a razor knife, cut the strips and number them on the back at the top edge so you can apply the strips in the proper sequence.

Pasting

With some wall coverings, you'll need to spread adhesive on the backing. Other coverings are pre-pasted; all you have to do is soak them in water before hanging them.

Unpasted wallpaper. Be sure to select the proper adhesive for your material (see "Choosing the Proper Adhesive," page 38).

If you're using a dry adhesive, mix it in a bucket according to the manufacturer's directions until it's smooth and not too thick. (If a few lumps remain, squish them between your thumb and forefinger.)

You'll need a wide, soft paint roller or pasting brush to apply paste to each strip. The goal in pasting is to cover the back of the wallpaper completely, smoothly, and evenly without smearing any paste on the pattern side.

To paste and book the strips, follow these steps:

1) Place the strips for one wall in the center of your work table, pattern side down. Align the first strip to be hung with the edge of the table.

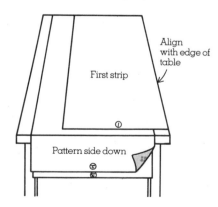

Align with edge of table

First strip

Pattern side down

2) Using a roller or brush, apply paste evenly to the back of the first strip. (Excess paste that laps over the edges will be caught by the back of the next strip.) Using an outward stroke, work from the center toward the edge. Be sure to apply enough paste to the edges.

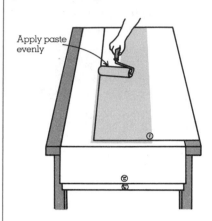

Apply paste evenly

3) To book the strip, fold the bottom third or more of the strip over the middle of the panel, pasted sides together, taking care not to crease the wallpaper sharply at the fold. Be sure the edges are aligned.

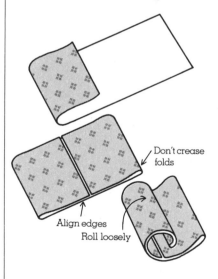

Don't crease folds

Align edges
Roll loosely

4) Fold over the remaining portion of the pasted strip until it meets the first cut end. Again, make sure the edges are aligned. Loosely roll booked strip and store it off the pasting table until you're ready to hang the strip.

5) If necessary, trim the selvage. To do this, place the pasted and booked strip (its edges aligned precisely) on the table. On one side,

align a straightedge with the trim marks. Using a razor knife, cut through both layers. Turn the strip around and follow the same procedure for the opposite side.

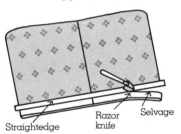

Straightedge

Razor knife

Selvage

You're now ready to hang the strip. For specific directions, see the step-by-step instructions on page 47.

Prepasted wallpaper. You'll need to soak this type of wall covering in water for the amount of time recommended by the manufacturer. Two techniques are described below. You may want to use the second one for a large room or for a wallpaper that stretches; it's also a good method for ensuring complete paste penetration.

For quickest application, follow these steps:

1) Place a water tray directly beneath the wall area the first strip will cover. Fill the tray half-full with lukewarm water.

2) Starting at the bottom of the cut strip, roll it up with the pattern side in.

THREE KINDS OF WALLPAPER SEAMS

Before hanging the second strip of wallpaper, you need to know how to select the right seam and how to make it. Following is a discussion of the three main types of wallpaper seams.

Butt seam. In most situations, the butt seam is the best way to join two strips of wallpaper, since it's the least noticeable seam. To make one, tightly butt the edge of the strip you're hanging to the edge of the previously hung strip. **Be very careful not to stretch the wallpaper.** Roll the seam (see page 47) to flatten it and prevent the edges from curling.

Lap seam. Commonly used for hanging wallpaper around an inside corner (rarely used on flat walls), the lap seam is made by lapping the edge of the strip being hung ½ inch or less over the edge of the previous hung strip.

Double cut seam. When a wall irregularity will cause the edge of the strip you're hanging to overlap the previously hung strip, make a double cut seam. To do this, complete the hanging of the second strip, disregarding the overlap. Immediately place a straightedge at the center of the overlap and, using a razor knife, cut through both layers of wallpaper. Remove the top cutoff section of the overlap. Carefully peel back the edge of the top strip until you can remove the bottom cut-off section. Smooth down the top strip; the seams should butt tightly together.

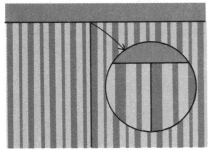

Butt seam

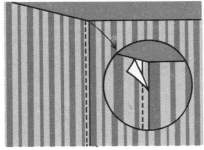

Lap seam

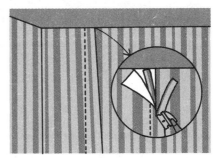

Double cut seam

---

3) Submerge the roll in the water tray for at least 30 seconds, depending on the manufacturer's specifications.

4) Grasp the top of the soaked strip and pull it up toward the ceiling; then follow the directions on page 47 for hanging the strip.

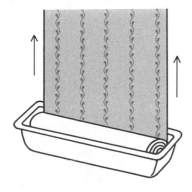

For a large room or a wallpaper that stretches, you can use the method that follows. This technique allows you to change the water as needed to get rid of paste residue and to maintain a lukewarm temperature; also, it prevents the wallpaper from tearing when lifted, from shrinking on the wall, and from curling at the edges.

1) Set up the water tray in your bathtub so you can change water when necessary.

2) Follow the directions above for soaking each strip.

3) After you pull the strip out of the water, place it, pattern side down, on a work table and book the strip.

4) Follow the directions on page 47 for hanging the strip.

HANGING THE FIRST STRIP

Whether you've applied adhesive or are using prepasted wallpaper, the procedure for hanging the strips is the same. For a helpful guide to applying wallpaper, see the illustrated sequence on page 47.

WHAT CAN GO WRONG?

If help is needed while you're hanging the first strip of wallpaper, it will probably be in one or more of these areas:

Air bubbles/blistering. Smooth out all air bubbles under each strip as you go. Minor ones will usually disappear when the strip is dry. Puncture stubborn air bubbles—particularly those under vinyl wall coverings—with a razor knife to release

Smooth out lumps with broad knife

trapped air. Use a broad knife to smooth out any paste lumps.

Misalignment. If a strip of wallpaper is wrinkling or not butting properly with the adjoining strip, chances are the strip isn't aligned correctly at the top. Don't try to force it or stretch it. Instead, gently pull off the strip and reposition it.

Loose edges. Pull the loose edge away from the wall just far enough to apply a thin coat of paste underneath with a small brush. Use a seam roller to press the edge firmly

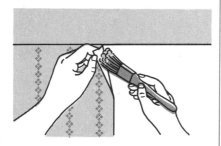

in place. Sponge off excess adhesive before it dries.

Curling edges. Some paper-backed vinyls have a tendency to curl at the edges. To prevent this, make sure to book each strip before hanging. In addition, see "Shop Talk" on page 44 for a good method of assuring proper paste penetration.

HANGING THE SECOND STRIP

Now that you've hung the first strip, your work will progress much more easily.

Paste your next strip, book it, and trim the selvages, if necessary. Unfold the strip on the wall in the same way you did the first. Gently butt the second strip against the first,

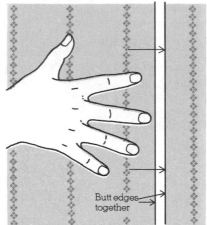

Butt edges together

aligning the pattern as you move down the wall. Smooth out the wallpaper with your brush, roll the seam, trim at the ceiling and baseboard, and wipe off excess paste.

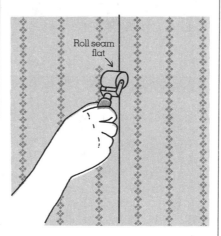

Roll seam flat

For textured wall coverings, such as grasscloth and burlap, it's sometimes advisable to reverse each strip for better color distribution. If one side of the covering happens to be shaded a little more heavily than the other, reversing strips will give a better finished appearance. Be sure to check the manufacturer's instructions before you do this.

Hang one strip pointing in an upward direction and the next strip

pointing downward (in relation to the way the material comes off the roll), butting dark edge to dark, light edge to light.

COVERING CORNERS

Covering inside and outside corners calls for special techniques. Here's how to handle each situation.

How to cover inside corners

Because few rooms have perfectly straight corners, you'll have to do some extra measuring for an exact fit at an inside corner. Start by measuring from the edge of the preceding strip to the corner; do this at three heights.

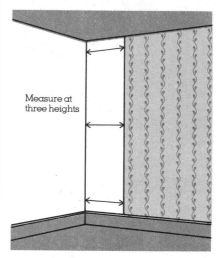

Measure at three heights

Cut a strip ½ inch wider than the widest measurement (don't discard the leftover piece of wallpaper; you'll use it to cover the adjacent side of the corner). Butting the strip

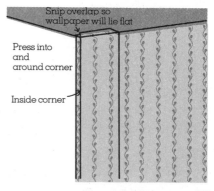

Snip overlap so wallpaper will lie flat

Press into and around corner

Inside corner

(Continued on page 48)

Hanging the First Strip

Step 1. Position step ladder next to plumb line (see page 42).

Step 2. Open top fold of strip, raising it so it overlaps ceiling line 2 inches.

Step 3. Carefully align strip's edge with plumb line.

Step 4. Using a smoothing brush, press strip against wall.

Step 5. Brush with a down-and-out stroke, moving from center of strip. Smooth out wrinkles and air bubbles.

Step 6. Release lower portion of strip and smooth into place.

Step 7. Using a seam roller, carefully roll edges flat, if necessary.

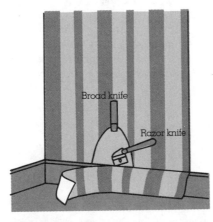

Step 8. Trim strip along ceiling and baseboard, using a broad knife and very sharp razor knife.

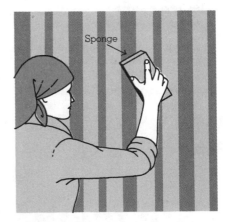

Step 9. Use a sponge dipped in luke-warm water to remove excess adhesive before it dries.

to the preceding strip, brush it firmly into and around the corner. At the top and bottom corners, cut the overlap so the strip will lie flat.

Measure the width of the leftover piece of wallpaper. On the adjacent wall, measure the same distance from the corner and make a plumb line (see page 42) at that point.

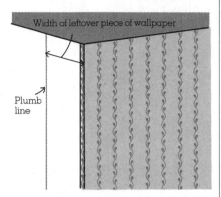

Depending on the direction you're going, position the correct edge of the strip along the plumb line; the other edge will cover the ½-inch overlap. (If you're using a nonporous wall covering, use a vinyl-to-vinyl adhesive on the ½-inch overlap.) This overlapping is necessary to keep the wall covering on the second wall plumb. The amount of pattern misalignment at the overlap is usually not noticeable.

How to cover outside corners

To hang a strip around an outside corner, butt the new strip to the previous strip and smooth as much of it as you can around the corner with-

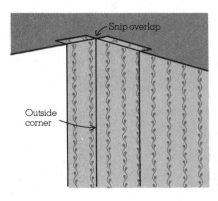

out buckling the wallpaper at the top and bottom corners. Snip the ceiling and baseboard overlaps precisely at each corner so that you can smooth the strip into place.

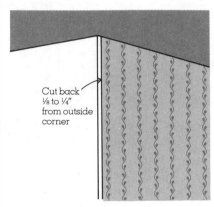

If a strip ends at an outside corner, cut it back ⅛ to ¼ inch. Wallpaper extended to the edge tends to fray or peel; the ⅛ to ¼-inch reduction won't be conspicuous. Wrap the next strip around the corner as described above.

WORKING AROUND OPENINGS

Caution: Before cutting around switches and outlets, you'll want to turn off the electricity.

Cutouts for electrical switches and outlets are easy to make. Be sure all faceplates have been removed before hanging the wall covering; then hang strips in the usual way, actually covering the opening. Use a razor knife to make an x-shaped cut over the opening, extending the cuts to each corner.

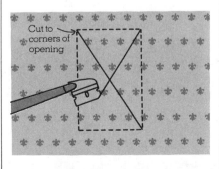

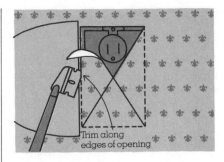

Trim the excess along the edges of the opening.

If you're hanging wallpaper around a small but immovable wall fixture such as a thermostat, smooth

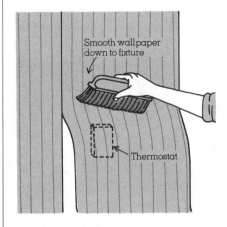

the strip as far down toward the fixture as you can; allow the remainder of the strip to drape over the fixture. Use a razor knife to cut a small x in the strip over the center of the fixture. Gradually make the hole bigger by carefully cutting around this x until you can smooth the strip into place; trim any excess.

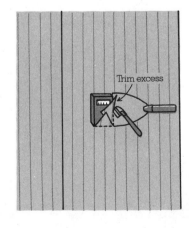

Papering around bulky immovable objects such as circular light fixture cover plates requires that you cut the strip so it can be smoothed down.

First, smooth the strip down toward the fixture, allowing the remainder of the strip to drape over the fixture. Then, starting at one edge, cut the strip to the center of the cover plate. Gradually cut away the strip in a circle until you can smooth the wallpaper around the plate. Finish smoothing out the strip, making sure the cut edges are butted tightly together. Trim any excess around the plate.

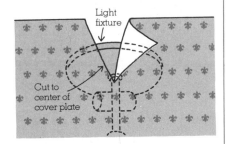

Light fixture

Cut to center of cover plate

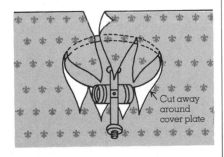

Cut away around cover plate

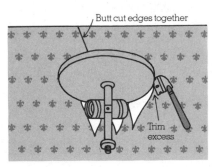

Butt cut edges together

Trim excess

Hanging wallpaper around doors, windows, and fireplaces won't seem as demanding if you think of these openings simply as larger electrical outlets. Don't try to custom fit large openings by meticulous measurement and advance cutting—there's an easier way.

Hang the strip as you normally would, but with the following difference: cut the excess material to within 2 inches of where you'll trim.

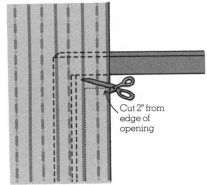

Cut 2" from edge of opening

Using shears, cut a 45° diagonal slit to the corners of the opening.

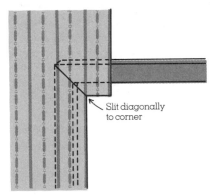

Slit diagonally to corner

Using a smoothing brush, press the wallpaper into place along all edges of the opening, pressing out air bubbles. Use a razor knife to trim excess material around the opening's frame, protecting the covering

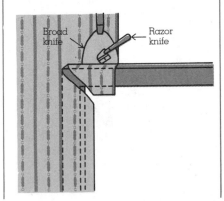

Broad knife

Razor knife

with a broad knife. Sponge off any excess paste.

To paper around recessed windows, see the illustrations below.

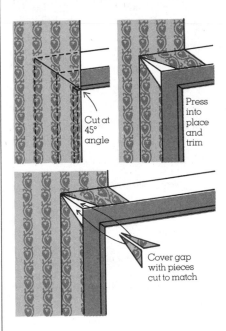

Cut at 45° angle

Press into place and trim

Cover gap with pieces cut to match

COVERING A CURVED ARCH

Hang the wallpaper above and around the arch normally, allowing the excess to hang freely. Cut the excess to within 2 inches of the bottom edge of the arch. Using shears,

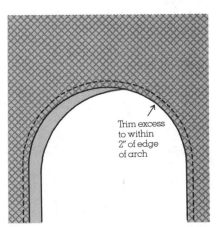

Trim excess to within 2" of edge of arch

make small, wedge-shaped cuts along the overlap, cutting as close to the edge of the arch as you can (see the illustration on page 50).

(Continued on next page)

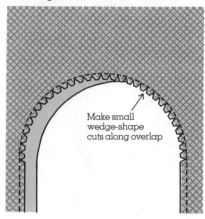

Make small wedge-shape cuts along overlap

Wrap the cut edges inside the arch (overlapping any pieces) and smooth them into place. Then, for the underside of the arch, cut a strip ⅛ inch narrower than the width of the arch (this prevents fraying or peeling). If your wall covering is nonporous, use vinyl-to-vinyl adhesive where the strips overlap under the arch.

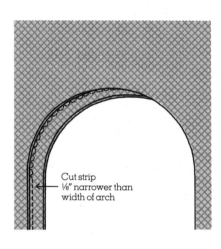

Cut strip ⅛" narrower than width of arch

DIFFERENT WALLPAPERS— DIFFERENT INSTALLATIONS

Some types of materials, such as vinyl, foil, flocked, woven, and fabric, call for special installation procedures. Follow the directions outlined below for the specific wall covering you're using, together with the basic directions for hanging all kinds of wall coverings beginning on page 45.

Vinyl

Because they're nonporous, vinyl wall coverings require a special vinyl adhesive. Wheat pastes can generate mildew problems when used with vinyl. Vinyl adhesive also helps keep strips from curling back from the wall along the edges.

Vinyl wall covering stretches if pulled. If it's stretched while being hung, the wall covering will shrink as it dries, causing hairline cracks at the seams. Booking your strips after pasting will eliminate this problem.

Some people prefer to use a vinyl squeegee instead of a smoothing brush for smoothing vinyl wall coverings. Always remove excess adhesive quickly from the face of this material before it dries.

Foil

Most manufacturers recommend hanging lining paper (see page 35) before installing foils. Lining paper not only creates a surface that will uniformly absorb excess moisture from the paste, but also provides a smooth wall surface.

Caution: Since it conducts electricity, avoid touching foil wallpaper to switches, receptacles, junction boxes, wiring, or any other electrical source. It's safest to turn off the electricity when hanging foil.

If you need to trim the selvages, place the dry strip, pattern side up, on a work table. Align a straightedge with the trim marks on one side. Holding the straightedge firmly in place, trim the selvage with a razor knife, using as few strokes as possible. Turn the strip around and trim the other edge.

To avoid scratches, creases, and folds (even slight creases or scratches can greatly impair the appearance of foil), roll up the strip, pattern side in.

To combat mildew and to provide strong adhesion, use a vinyl adhesive, never a wheat paste. Apply paste to the wall (unless the wallpaper manufacturer specifies differently), being careful not to overpaste (see above right).

Apply paste to wall

Unroll each strip onto the wall, smoothing the foil into place vertically (not side to side) to avoid warping and curling at the edges.

Since foil neither contracts nor expands appreciably when dry, you must eliminate air bubbles immediately. If they can't be smoothed out, puncture them carefully and press them down.

Oriental weaves & natural textures

These nonwashable materials are generally laminated to a paper backing that can be loosened if you apply too much adhesive. Covering the wall first with lining paper (see page 35) will help absorb moisture from the adhesive.

Butt seams by pushing the strips gently with the palms of your hands. Then smooth the material with a smoothing brush; don't rub the surface with your hands. To avoid crushing the texture, use only light pressure when rolling the seams.

These materials may be difficult to cut when wet. For best results, wait until the adhesive has dried before trimming the ceiling and baseboard edges.

Remove excess paste by wiping gently or blotting with a damp sponge.

Flocked wallpaper

When hanging this material, it's important to keep adhesive off the flocked surface and not to crush the flocking.

After you've pasted and booked a strip, allow it to sit long enough to become limp. Then use a soft, natural bristle brush for pressing and smoothing it onto the wall; avoid overbrushing. To lay the nap in the

Brush upward to lay nap.

same direction, finish with upward strokes.

To roll seams flat, glue a scrap of flocked wallpaper over the roller head; press lightly on the seams to flatten them and prevent curling edges.

Though flocks are nearly always washable, remove any paste that does get on the surface very gently.

Fabric wallpaper

Use premixed vinyl adhesive to install fabrics laminated to paper backing. Trim all selvages before hanging. Then spread paste on the fabric's backing and hang, butting edges. To prevent staining, keep adhesive off the fabric surface. If you have to sponge off excess adhesive, avoid soaking—it will curl the fabric.

HOW TO HANDLE A CEILING

Hanging wallpaper on the ceiling can give your room an entirely new look. It can be a continuation of a pattern on the walls, or the only surface in the room that's papered.

For best results, choose a random allover pattern that coordinates with the pattern on the walls. This avoids the need to match patterns where the walls and ceiling meet, as well as the upside-down match you'd get along one ceiling line if you used a one-way pattern.

Paper the ceiling *before* you cover the walls. When measuring the dimensions of the ceiling, plan to run the strips across the shorter distance; this way, they'll be much more manageable.

To find the square footage of the ceiling, multiply the length of the room by the width. See page 37 to determine how many rolls of wallpaper you'll need to cover the surface.

Prepare the ceiling surface in the same manner as you did the walls (see page 38) and remove all fixtures. Cut, paste, and book the strips (see page 43), allowing 2 inches extra length at each end of the strips and a ½-inch overlap at each side wall edge, as shown below.

Work with a ladder, or better yet, create a simple

scaffold by placing a plank between two ladders, as shown below.

Before you can hang the first strip, you'll need to establish plumb. To do this, measure in from the ceiling corner ½ inch less than the width of the wallpaper. Mark the ceiling at that point. Move to the far end of the wall and measure in the same distance from the corner; mark the ceiling at this point also. Tack a string rubbed with chalk to the ceiling at both of these marks and snap a chalk line between them.

To hang the wallpaper, follow the steps on page 47. Techniques for seams are on page 45; to work around fixtures, see page 49. The hanging process will be much easier if you have a helper. One person can align and smooth the wallpaper while the other holds the remaining length up and out of the way with a broom or other soft-edged tool, as shown below.

If you don't plan to paper the walls, you'll need to trim the 2-inch overlap on the ceiling; use a razor knife cutting along the edges where the ceiling and walls meet. If you're covering the walls as well, trim the overlap to ½ inch. When you hang the wall strips, use double-cut seams at the ceiling lines to prevent gaps at the seam lines.

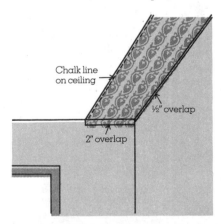

Chalk line on ceiling

½" overlap

2" overlap

USING BORDERS

Sometimes, a decorative border can add the perfect finishing touch to your project. Though borders are generally used along the ceiling lines, they can be used anywhere you want a distinct break between materials.

If the border has a distinct pattern, you may want to plan its application. Center the pattern on the wall and work out to each corner; use a separate piece of border paper for each wall.

Use a vinyl-to-vinyl paste for any type of border you plan to hang over wallpaper. To paste the border for hanging, cover the entire back with paste and book the strip; don't crease the folds.

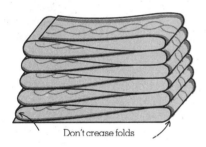

Don't crease folds

To hang the border, begin at the least conspicuous corner. The work will go much faster if you have someone hold the folded section while you apply the border to the

Border

wall. Take care not to drip paste onto the wall and be sure to remove excess paste.

Use your fingers to press the border into corners; avoid crease

marks. Because the border is narrow, it's not necessary to be concerned about how straight the corners are. Just work the border into the corner and continue around the room.

PROTECTING & CLEANING WALLPAPER

Considering the time, energy, and expense of hanging a wall covering, you'll understandably want it to last. Protect and clean it according to the guidelines that follow.

Protecting wallpaper

You can apply a protective coating to a nonvinyl wallpaper to make it easier to clean and prolong its life. Ask your dealer to suggest the right coating to use with your material.

It's a good idea to use a protective coating in heavy-traffic areas, especially hallways and children's rooms. Though the coating changes the covering's color slightly, it dries clear and is washable. Don't apply a protective coating until the paste is completely dry (it takes about a week).

Cleaning wallpaper

Most wallpapers come with cleaning instructions; read them carefully and file them for future reference. If you can't remove stains, you can patch the damaged area (see "Shop Talk," above right).

Below are some other helpful hints for cleaning your wallpaper.

Cleaning with commercial dough. This material removes dirt and grime from both washable and nonwashable coverings; it's not effective against stains. Apply cleaning dough to entire walls or rooms, not just on spots.

When using the dough, begin at the top of the wall and work down, using long, light strokes. Avoid streaking by making all strokes in the same direction. As the cleaning dough becomes soiled, it

must be kneaded until clean. After you've finished cleaning, wipe the surface with a clean rag to remove any dough.

Removing stains on washable wallpaper. To remove dirt, grease, and stains before they can penetrate the wallpaper, thoroughly wash the soiled area with a mild soap and cold water solution. Rinse with clear, cold water. Wipe dry with a clean, absorbent cloth.

Removing stains on nonwashable wallpaper. To clean stains from nonwashable wallpaper, use a sponge moistened with a mild soap and cold water solution. Carefully blot only the soiled area. Then blot the soap solution with a sponge moistened only with clear, cold water. Blot the section dry with a clean, absorbent cloth.

Removing stains with commercial spot removers. You can buy commercial spot removers that will eradicate stains from some types of wallpaper. Ask your dealer to recommend the proper spot remover for your material and follow the directions carefully.

FABRIC
FOR ONE-OF-A-KIND WALLS

Walk into any room with fabric walls and you'll be surprised at the dramatic effect they impart. From canvas to linen, bold prints to petite country florals, formal designs to solid colors, fabric on the walls adds texture and warmth to your room. Best of all, you don't have to be an expert at sewing. All you need to achieve professional results are careful measurements and a steady hand.

Underlying its apparent beauty, each fabric application—upholstered, stapled, shirred, and pasted—has functional characteristics to consider. Insulating, soundproofing, and concealing irreparable cracks are benefits of shirred, stapled, and especially upholstered walls. In rooms where steam is a factor, fabric pasted to walls is the best choice, because it won't curl at the edges or deteriorate, and spots can be easily removed.

Step-by-step instructions will lead you from beginning to end of each installation, getting you around every corner and finishing every edge. In this chapter you'll also find several helpful features, such as the one on "Yardage Arithmetic," that will guide you victoriously through the battle of numbers to determine the amount of fabric to buy.

GUIDELINES FOR SELECTING FABRIC

Using fabric to cover your walls can significantly change the mood and feeling of your room. Choose a fabric and pattern that will both enhance your possessions and express your taste.

Choose firmly woven fabrics that have strength and stability in both the lengthwise and crosswise directions. Loosely woven fabrics, such as tweed, will unravel and stretch out of shape on a wall. Silk, linen, and very lightweight cotton fabrics stain easily and attract dust, so they're not recommended for rooms that receive hard wear.

Upholstery fabrics are an excellent choice. Available in widths up to 60 inches, they're usually treated with a repellent that inhibits stains and dust collection. In addition, these fabrics are printed with pattern overlaps at the selvages, making it easy to match the pattern at the seams.

Also consider using flat bed sheets—these are suitable for all applications except pasting, where their size makes them hard to handle. Less expensive than upholstery fabric, sheets are made from tightly woven fabric in widths up to 108 inches. See "Shop Talk" on page 61 for information on sheet sizes.

(Continued on next page)

Be cautious when selecting a printed fabric. Generally, the print will be slightly off-grain—veering at an angle from the lengthwise and crosswise threads. Often, the misalignment isn't noticeable. But if it is, don't use the fabric, since it won't hang properly.

To check patterned fabric, fold it back a few inches along the horizontal grain, wrong sides together, aligning selvages. If the print runs evenly along the fold, it's fairly well aligned with the grain. If the print wanders across the fold, it's badly off-grain.

Fabrics with allover designs show less soil than those with large, open-ground patterns. Allover patterns can help camouflage wall textures and imperfections, uneven ceiling lines, and mistakes in application.

UPHOLSTERING WALLS

Like upholstered furniture, walls covered with fabric over padding add an air of sophistication to a room and display fine workmanship. Batting underneath the fabric pads the walls, enhances the insulating and acoustic features of the fabric wall, and gives the fabric a soft, cushioned appearance.

To upholster a wall, you first staple batting to the wall. Then you seam fabric panels together into a fabric cover—you'll need a separate one for each wall you're upholstering. You staple the outer edges of the fabric cover to the wall over the layer of batting, then cover the staples and fabric edges with trim (see page 59).

If you want to upholster the ceiling as well, do it before you cover the walls; follow the same procedure as for the walls.

Polyester batting usually won't deteriorate or decay during the life of your fabric wall. But upholstered walls are not recommended for kitchens and bathrooms where steam and grease stains can damage fabric and batting fibers.

You'll also want to consider the type of wall you have. Test the wall to see if stapling will damage it. In many cases, the small holes left by the staples can be easily filled with paint or a coat of spackle if you decide to remove the fabric later on.

If the staples can't puncture the surface, or if they leave large holes and chip the wall surface, mount furring strips (see page 88) to provide a working surface.

EQUIPMENT & SUPPLIES

The most important piece of equipment you'll need is a **staple gun**, along with a full box of **⅜-inch staples**.

An electric staple gun will speed your work and prevent aching arms and fingers, but because most electric guns have their motors at the head, you can't use them along the ceiling line (unless there's a ceiling molding) or in corners. For this close work, you'll need a handheld staple gun.

A **tack hammer** may come in handy for tapping in any staples that don't penetrate deeply enough. You'll need cardboard **tack strips** to hold the stapled fabric securely and maintain sharp edges in corners. You can purchase strips in an upholstery shop; buy enough stripping to run the height of the wall for all inside corners to be covered.

A **steel tape measure,** more accurate than a fabric tape, is an essential tool. **Craft glue** is used to apply trim to fabric edges and adhere fabric to faceplates (spray adhesive can be substituted on faceplates).

Also have a **staple remover, fabric shears, long push pins** (the ¾-inch size available in stationery stores), a **razor knife, utility razor blades** (the type available in hardware stores), and a **broad knife** or metal straightedge.

When you staple along the ceiling line, use a **stepladder** that's taller than the height at which you need to stand to reach the ceiling comfortably. Or you can make a simple scaffold (see page 51). A **sewing machine** is necessary if you need to stitch lengths of fabric together. Use an **iron** to remove fabric creases and press seams open.

DETERMINING YARDAGE

Making accurate measurements of the wall surfaces you're covering is the first step in determining how much fabric, batting, and trim you'll need. If you follow the instructions below and the procedure illustrated in the special feature, "Yardage Arithmetic" (facing page), you can't go wrong in your calculations. Before you make your purchases, take time to check and recheck the total yardage figures required for each material.

These figures include a margin of safety that will ensure you'll have enough material to complete the project. Often, the same pattern or dye lot isn't available later.

How to measure for fabric

Use a long steel tape to measure the wall. You'll want to mark the dimensions on a piece of paper, since you'll use the figures to make the yardage calculations (see "Yardage Arithmetic," facing page) and to determine cutting lines later. As you measure, keep in mind that each wall is to be covered with a separate fabric cover.

Width measurement. Measure separately the width (in inches) of each wall you're planning to cover, unless you'll be working around an outside corner (see page 48). In this case, you'll use one fabric cover, starting it at one wall edge, wrapping it around the corner, and continuing to the far edge of the wall.

To find the number of fabric panels required for one wall, divide the width of the wall by the usable width of the fabric, taking into account the amount of fabric taken up in seams (allow ½-inch seam allowances).

If your calculations result in a fraction, round up to the next whole number of fabric panels. This extra fabric width will give you some leeway to match patterns at wall corners.

Height measurement. Measure the height (in inches) of the same wall from the ceiling line (or lower edge of the ceiling molding) to the top of the baseboard. Take this measure-

YARDAGE ARITHMETIC

Outlined below are instructions for measuring for fabric, batting, and trim. Use the sample room measurements as a model for your own calculations to determine how much yardage you'll need for your upholstered wall project.

Using the directions in "Determining Yardage" (see facing page), take accurate measurements of the dimensions of the area you plan to cover with fabric.

In the example below, three walls are being upholstered. Make whatever adjustments are necessary for the number of walls you're covering. For stapled walls, follow the calculations below for fabric and trim.

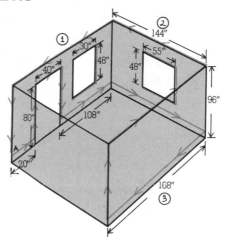

Fabric

Walls 1 and 3

Step 1: width of wall ÷ (fabric width − 1″ for seams) = number of fabric panels needed, rounded off to next whole number

$168″ ÷ 53″ = 3.2 = 4$

Step 2: height + "insurance" + pattern repeat = working height of wall

$96″ + 6″ + 8″ = 110″$

Step 3: working height × number of panels = length of fabric needed, converted to yards

$110″ × 4 = 440″ = 12¼$ yards

Wall 2

Step 1: $144″ ÷ 53″ = 2.6 = 3$
Step 2: $96″ + 6″ + 8″ = 110″$
Step 3: $110″ × 3 = 330″ = 9¼$ yards

Total fabric required

fabric for wall 1 + wall 2 + wall 3 = total fabric yardage required

$12¼$ yards $+ 9¼$ yards $+ 12¼$ yards $= 33¾$ yards

Batting

Step 1: width of wall 1 + width of wall 2 + width of wall 3 = total width of walls

$168″ + 144″ + 168″ = 480″$

Step 2: width of walls ÷ batting width = number of widths needed, rounded off to next whole number

$480″ ÷ 54″ = 8.8 = 9$

Step 3: number of widths × wall height = batting length subtotal, converted to yards

$9 × 8′ = 72′ = 24$ yards

Step 4: batting subtotal − measurement of large opening (Wall 2 window) = total batting yardage required

24 yards $− 1$ yard $= 23$ yards

Trim

Step 1: Starting at Point A and following red arrow, add all wall and connected opening measurements along path:

Wall 1	$20″ + 80″ + 40″ + 80″ + 108″$	$= 328″$
Wall 2		$= 144″$
Wall 3	$168″ + 96″ + 168″$	$= 432″$
Wall 2		$= 144″$
Wall 1	$168″ + 96″$	$= 264″$
		TOTAL 1352″

Step 2: measure around separate openings

Wall 1 window = $(48″ × 2) + (30″ × 2)$	$= 156″$
Wall 2 window = $(48″ × 2) + (55″ × 2)$	$= \underline{206″}$
	$362″$

Step 3: $1312″ + 362″ = 1674″ = 46.5$ yards $= 47$ yards

total from Step 1 + total from Step 2 = total trim required, converted to yards and rounded off to next whole number ment in several places to check for variations caused by settling; use the largest figure.

Add 6 inches to the height measurement as insurance against errors. If the fabric has a pattern repeat, add the repeat length to the height measurement to allow for matching the pattern at the seams. Your final figure is the working height of the wall.

Total fabric yardage. Multiply the working height figure by the number of fabric panels needed for the wall; convert to yards to determine the number of running yards of fabric required for the one wall you've measured (see page 55).

Repeat the calculations outlined above for each wall you're covering. Add together the running yards for all the walls to determine the total fabric yardage you need.

Batting basics & measurements

To pad the walls, use ¾-inch bonded polyester batting. Available either 27 or 54 inches wide, batting can be purchased in upholstery fabric shops or custom furniture shops.

To compute the amount of batting you'll need, measure (in inches) the exact height and width of the area to be covered; *do not* add extra inches.

Add the width measurements of all the walls together and divide by the width of the batting to determine how many strips of batting you need; round off to the next larger whole number. Multiply this figure by the height of the wall and convert to yards to compute how much batting is required.

Dimensions of large openings, such as sliding doors and picture windows, can be subtracted from your yardage figure, since batting can be pieced around openings.

Trim selection & measurement

Trim provides a professional finish to an upholstered wall by covering staples and raw edges of fabric.

Double welt made from the same fabric as the wall or a complementary fabric is the traditional finish (to make double welt, see page 60). You can also use braid, gimp, or grosgrain ribbon in the same or a contrasting color for a different effect. Molding—stained, painted, or wrapped with fabric—also makes an attractive trim.

Plan to use a continuous strip of trim (unless you're using molding) without piecing for the perimeter of the area to be covered. To determine how much trim you'll need, track in your mind a course that starts at an inconspicuous corner, travels around the perimeter of the upholstered area, and finishes back at the starting point without any break (see page 55).

Measure this distance and round up to the next half-yard figure to provide a margin of safety. Also measure around the edges of all unconnected openings, such as windows, that must be trimmed. Add all measurements together to determine the total yardage required.

PREPARING THE FABRIC & BATTING

Before you begin the work of upholstering the walls, you'll need to prepare the fabric covers and cut the batting to size for each wall.

Cutting & stitching the fabric

If the fabric has an allover print, it's not necessary to plan where the seams will hang on the wall. Once the fabric is stretched over the wall, seams won't show. But if you're using a solid color fabric, seams will be noticeable, so you'll want to plan their placement carefully (see "Where to begin," page 42).

Cutting the fabric. Spread the fabric out on a flat, smooth surface. Using tailor's chalk or a pencil, mark the point on the pattern that will lie

along the ceiling line. From that point down, measure and mark the length of the first strip according to the height measurements you recorded (see page 55).

Cut straight across the fabric at the top and bottom markings. Continue cutting fabric panels, matching patterns if necessary, until you have enough to cover *one* wall. Make sure the panels run in the same direction; reversing the nap can produce color variation that may be apparent only after the fabric is upon the wall.

If you're using a light-colored fabric with printing (such as the manufacturer's name or color keys) on the selvages, cut them off.

To avoid confusion, stitch together the panels you've just cut for the first fabric cover before continuing to the remaining fabric. Be sure the pattern placement at the ceiling line is the same for all subsequent fabric panels you cut.

Stitching the seams. Pin the fabric panels, right sides together, matching patterns. Using ½-inch seam allowances and starting at the top edge, stitch the panels; backstitch at the beginning and end of each seam. Press the seams open and press out any creases.

Cutting the batting

Measure strips of batting in lengths equal to the height of the wall. Cut enough strips to cover the entire area you're upholstering; you'll fit the batting for width when you apply the batting.

UPHOLSTERING THE WALLS

Now you're ready to hang the batting and the fabric covers according to the directions that follow; on page 58 you'll find these directions illustrated. At the end of this section are instructions for working around openings, covering narrow spaces, and applying trim.

Remember that if you're upholstering the ceiling, you need to do it before you cover the walls. Upholster the ceiling as you would a wall.

Work from the left to right around the room (unless you're left-handed, in which case you may find it more comfortable to work from right to left).

You'll need to remove everything from the walls. *Caution:* Before unscrewing faceplates from switches and outlets, turn off the electricity to prevent accidents when you're working around electrical openings.

Hanging the batting

It's best to start in the least conspicuous corner or at the edge of an opening that runs from floor to ceiling.

Position the first strip of batting ¾ inch away from the wall and ceiling edges. You'll use this ¾-inch space to staple the fabric cover to the wall. If batting is caught in the staples holding the fabric, the staples will cause dents or ridges to appear when the fabric is stretched across the wall.

Placing the staples at least an inch in from the edge of the batting and about a foot apart, staple the batting strips along the ceiling line. (Don't staple along the edge of the batting, or dents will appear.) Staple down the left side, then down the right side of the batting.

Cut any excess off the bottom edge, leaving a ¾-inch space between batting and baseboard; staple across the bottom.

The batting should be ¾ inch away from each inside corner; wrap batting around outside corners (see page 48). Cut the batting ¾ inch away from the edges of all openings, except outlets and switches. These will be covered with faceplates, so carefully cut the batting just to the edge of the opening.

Butt the second batting strip against the first and staple across the top edge. Then staple down the left side and the right side of the second strip (see Step 1, page 58). Cut excess batting from the bottom and staple. Continue until the entire area is covered with batting.

Stapling the first fabric wall

Position the fabric cover so the left side hangs down the edge of the wall and the top edge of the fabric is aligned with the ceiling line. Holding the fabric along the ceiling line and working from left to right, use push pins to pin the fabric in place along the ceiling line for 3 to 4 feet; let the remaining fabric hang freely.

Starting at the top and working down, staple the left side of the fabric, positioning the staples parallel to the wall edge and about the width of a staple apart from each other (see Step 2, page 58). The staples must be close together so the fabric won't ripple when it's pulled taut.

Return to the ceiling line and staple the fabric that's being held with push pins. Then, holding the remaining fabric in your right hand, extend your arm to the right as far as you can reach; staple the fabric in place at that point.

Staple the top edge of the fabric from left to right, as shown in Step 3, page 58, until you reach the far staple. Repeat the procedure to the end of the wall. When working around an outside corner, continue stapling as described, pulling the fabric taut around the corner.

Checking for plumb. With the left wall and top edge of the fabric cover in place, check that seams are straight. Hang a plumb line down the seam that's farthest right (see "Establishing plumb," page 42). Straighten the seam by pulling the fabric taut at the bottom edge; staple the lower edge of the fabric at the seamline to hold it in place.

Check the seams to the left—they should be straight. Staple the lower edge of each seam in place.

Stapling the inside corner

If you're upholstering only one wall and not working around any inside corners, proceed to "Finishing the bottom edge," at right. But if you're upholstering walls with inside corners, follow these directions. The process is slow, but the results are worth the extra effort.

Stretch the fabric around the inside corner. Using staple gun pressure and your hand to pull the fabric taut to the second wall, staple the fabric to the second wall from top to bottom as far into the corner as possible (see Step 4, page 58). Insert staples parallel to the corner edge; don't catch batting in the staples.

Using push pins, tack the fabric cover for the second wall along the ceiling line of the first wall, right sides together (see Step 5, page 58). To match fabric patterns, align the edge of the second fabric cover to the pattern of the first cover. Use the vertical line in the pattern or the fabric grainline to ensure that patterns are matched all the way down the wall.

Staple the second fabric cover at several points in the corner down the second wall; as you staple, remove the push pins and flip the fabric over to check pattern alignment. Remove staples and make adjustments, if necessary. Trim any excess fabric from the corner.

Push a tack strip tightly into the corner on the second wall, as shown in Step 5, page 58. Staple the tack strip in place over both fabric layers; the strip will hold the fabric tightly in place and make a smooth, flat corner edge.

Butt a second tack strip to the bottom of the first and staple it into place; don't overlap the strips. Apply additional strips, if necessary, in the same manner; use shears to trim the bottom strip to fit. Remove the push pins, bring the second fabric cover over to the second wall, and pin it 3 to 4 feet along the ceiling line.

Finishing the bottom edge

Staple the bottom edge of the first fabric cover, keeping staples as close to the baseboard as possible (see Step 6, page 58).

Protecting the fabric cover with a broad knife or metal straightedge, use a razor knife to cut excess fabric along the baseboard. Keep the

(Continued on page 59)

Upholstering a Wall

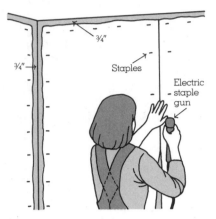

Step 1. Staple batting strips ¾" from all edges, butting adjacent strips.

Step 2. Pin fabric to ceiling line with push pins. Staple down left side of fabric; don't catch batting in staples.

Step 3. Pull fabric taut to right along ceiling line; staple from left to right close to ceiling line.

Step 4. Establish plumb to keep pattern straight. Holding fabric taut, staple in corner along second wall.

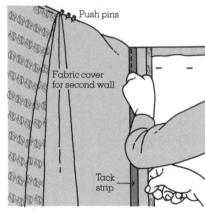

Step 5. Pin fabric for second wall over first wall, right sides together. Matching patterns, staple edge of second fabric cover in corner. Push tack strips into corner; staple.

Step 6. Staple fabric to wall along baseboard. Using broad knife to protect fabric cover, cut excess fabric with razor knife.

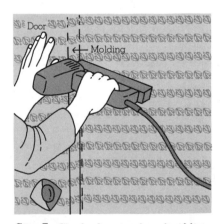

Step 7. Staple close to edge of molding around openings. Carefully cut holes for corners and door knobs.

Step 8. Using razor knife, trim excess fabric from opening along edge of molding. Protect fabric with broad knife.

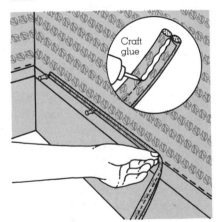

Step 9. Apply craft glue to underside of welt. Using push pins, tack welt in place along edge of fabric cover.

razor blade flat against the wall; change blades frequently to avoid pulled and stretched fabric edges.

If you're covering only one wall, finish the edge according to the directions below.

Stapling the second wall

Extend the second fabric cover to the right as far as you can reach, and staple it in place along the ceiling line. Continue stapling, following the procedure for the first fabric cover.

Taking care to match patterns and form sharp corners, attach the remaining fabric covers in the same manner.

Finishing the last wall edge

The way you staple the last side of the fabric cover depends on the type of wall edge you've reached.

If you have worked around the room and have come back to the first wall, staple the last fabric side to the first wall over the staples where you began. Carefully cut excess fabric away with fabric shears. Later you'll glue trim over these staples to finish the edge.

If the final fabric side is along the edge of a floor-to-ceiling opening, staple the fabric close to the edge of the wall. Cut excess fabric away with a razor knife.

Covering narrow spaces

A strip of wall that's less than 4 inches wide is very difficult to upholster using the method just described. Instead, cut a piece of poster board to fit the space. Using no batting, wrap the fabric around

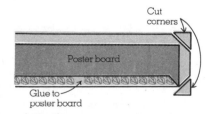

Cut corners

Poster board

Glue to poster board

the poster board and glue the edges in place on the back, as shown. Using brads, tack the covered strip to the wall; poke the nail heads under the fabric.

Working around openings

At this point in your project, you may notice that all the doors and windows have been hidden under fabric. To expose them and let the sunlight in, follow these directions.

Starting at the bottom edge of the molding, staple the fabric to the wall as close to the molding as possible (see Step 7, page 58); don't catch batting in the staples. As you staple, cut holes for door knobs and molding corners to pop through so you can keep the fabric taut across the wall surface.

When stapling is completed, use a razor knife to cut the fabric along the molding edge, protecting the fabric with a broad knife as shown in Step 8, page 58.

Covering faceplates

You can cover switch and outlet faceplates with fabric to match the wall. We recommend craft glue for this—spray contact cement can also be used, but it dries in a yellow color, so it's not satisfactory for light-colored fabrics.

Caution: Before you begin, be sure the electricity is turned off.

Find the wall opening by feel and carefully cut the fabric cover along the edges of the opening. Spread glue on the faceplate and position it over the opening. Place a scrap of fabric over it, matching its pattern to the pattern on the wall.

Take the faceplate off the wall and smooth the fabric in place. Trim within ½ inch of the edge of the faceplate and cut away the corners. Razor-cut along the edges of the openings on the faceplate and punch holes at the screw openings. Trim any loose threads.

Apply a thin strip of glue to the back edges of the faceplate, wrap

the fabric around, and press it in place. Cut away excess fabric.

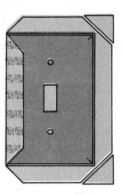

Applying trim

Applying trim is the easiest part of installing a fabric wall. Double welt, braid, gimp, grosgrain ribbon, and molding all provide a professional-looking finish to your project.

Double welt. Make one continuous strip of double welt (for directions, see page 60), or have it made professionally.

Plan to start applying the welt a few inches from a corner along the baseboard. This enables you to get the feel of the technique while you're working in an inconspicuous area.

Apply a 12-inch-long strip of craft glue to the underside (side with raw edge) of the welt along the center stitching line. Place the welt along the bottom edge of the fabric cover with the raw edge facing toward the baseboard. Tack the trim in place with push pins as shown in Step 9, page 58.

Repeat the procedure for the next section of welt.

To work around corners, press the welt firmly and tightly into place. Long push pins come in handy here to hold the welt securely until the glue dries.

To finish the ends, cut the welt so it's an inch longer than the area remaining to be covered. Push the welt fabric back to expose both cords; cut an inch off the ends of both cords. Fold the welt fabric ½ inch to the wrong side; spread with glue. Apply the remaining welt to the wall with the cordless fabric overlapping the first welt end.

Braid, gimp, or ribbon. Apply these trims in the same manner as double welt. If the braid is too bulky to turn under, cut the edge so it butts against the first braid end. Use craft glue to keep the edges from fraying.

Molding. Molding (see page 95) can be stained, painted, or covered with fabric. To cover with fabric, wrap a fabric strip around the molding; glue the edges in place on the wrong side.

Using brads, tack the molding to the wall at the edge of the fabric cover.

Fabric care

To prevent stains, treat the walls with a stain repellent. On all fabric walls, you can spray the fabric after installation; be sure to follow the manufacturer's instructions. For normal cleaning, vacuum the walls.

STAPLING FABRIC TO WALLS

Stapling fabric to a wall is easy and quick.

You stitch together panels of fabric in the same way as for upholstered walls and install the fabric covers similarly. But you don't have to work over batting or place the staples quite so close together. Also, you use a simple technique around corners. (Complete instructions on upholstering walls begin on page 56.)

To simulate the appearance of upholstered walls and significantly increase insulating and acoustic qualities, choose a quilted fabric.

EQUIPMENT & SUPPLIES

A **staple gun** is a must, as is a large box of **⅜-inch staples** (½-inch staples for quilted fabrics). Also have

---

MAKING YOUR OWN DOUBLE WELT

Double welt adds the same fine finish to fabric walls as it does to upholstered furniture. Use it to decoratively cover fabric raw edges and staples.

Materials you'll need

To determine the amount of welt you'll need, see how to measure trim, page 56. Purchase **¼-inch cord** *twice* the length of the trim measurement.

Make the casing for the cord from fabric strips cut on the bias. You'll need enough 1¾-inch-wide bias strips to make a welt equal to the trim measurement.

Use the following guidelines for purchasing **fabric:** if your fabric is 36 inches wide, purchase 1 yard of fabric for every 18 yards of welt you need. If your fabric is 45 inches wide, buy 1 yard of fabric for every 23 yards of welt you're making. For 54-inch-wide fabric, you'll need 1 yard of fabric for every 28 yards of welt.

You'll also need a **sewing machine** with a zipper foot, a **tape measure,** a **straightedge,** and **tailor's chalk** or a pencil.

Stitching the welt

Cut enough bias strips to make the welt and stitch them together, using a ¼-inch seam allowance. Or you can make a continuous bias casing. For directions, see either of these *Sunset* books: *How to Make Pillows* or *Slipcovers & Bedspreads.*

Wrap one edge of the casing around a piece of cord, leaving a ⅛ to ¼-inch flap of fabric as shown. Using the zipper foot, stitch close to the cord down the entire length of the casing.

On the wrong side of the fabric next to the stitching line, place the second piece of cord. Wrap the fabric over the cord.

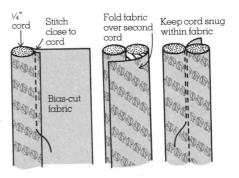

Turn the welt to the front. Using the regular presser foot, stitch over the first stitching line as shown; hold the fabric securely so the cords stay close together and are tightly bound.

An alternate method is to purchase double welt cording, two pieces of cording stitched together. Wrap the bias casing around the cords, as described above, omitting the first row of stitching. With the front side up, stitch down the center of the double welt, holding the fabric securely so the cords are tightly bound.

on hand a **steel tape measure, fabric shears, razor knife, utility razor blades, broad knife** or metal straightedge, **staple remover,** and **stepladder.** If you need to stitch panels of fabric together, you'll want a **sewing machine** and **iron.**

WALL & FABRIC PREPARATION

If you need to use furring strips, install them according to the directions on page 88.

Measure and prepare the fabric covers following the instructions on pages 54–56.

STAPLING FROM START TO FINISH

To staple the fabric covers to the wall, follow the same progression as for upholstered walls (see page 56): left side, ceiling line, right side, and bottom edge. Place staples 2 to 3 inches apart.

Corners of stapled walls are easy to handle. Simply stretch the fabric for the first wall to the corner and staple it to the first wall as far into the corner as possible. Protecting the fabric with a broad knife, use a razor knife to trim excess fabric (see Step 8, page 58).

Start the second wall fabric cover in the same manner as you started the first wall, matching the pattern as closely as possible. Staple all edges as shown below. To work around openings, see page 59.

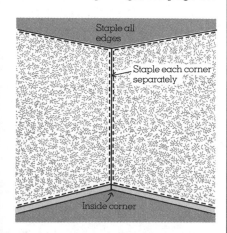

Staple all edges

Staple each corner separately

Inside corner

Cover the staples and raw edges with trim (molding, welt, ribbon, gimp, or braid) when all walls are stapled. To determine trim length, see page 56, but remember to add twice the wall height measurement to your total for each corner that must be covered (you need to cover the raw edges and staples on both sides of every corner).

To apply the trim, see page 59.

For care instructions, see "Fabric care" on page 59.

SHIRRED FABRIC WALLS

A shirred wall treatment—a gathered curtain on rods attached to the wall along the ceiling and baseboard edges—is a perfect way to cover uneven or damaged surfaces, pipes or ducts, even windows that look out on brick walls. It can mean a new lease on life for apartment walls that can't be modified by tenants.

A shirred wall can be installed with a minimum of time, effort, and sewing skill; even imperfect seams are well hidden in the folds of the fabric. But keep in mind that you'll need at least twice as much fabric for this method as for any other technique.

EQUIPMENT & SUPPLIES

To hang the fabric, you'll need **cafe curtain rods** for the top and bottom of each wall you're covering, as well as at the top and bottom of all openings, and **brackets** to support the rods. If you're covering an entire wall, brackets must be hung every few feet to provide support.

To prepare the fabric, you'll want a **sewing machine, fabric shears,** and **steel tape measure.** Use an **iron** to press side edges, hems, and casings.

DETERMINING YARDAGE

The fullness of the gathers in a shirred wall depends on the weight of the fabric. Lightweight fabrics look best with fullness 2½ times the width of the wall; heavier fabrics look best with fullness about twice the width of the wall.

Measure the width of the wall and multiply by the amount of desired fullness. Divide the total by the fabric's width to determine how many panels of fabric are needed.

To determine the length required for each panel, measure the height of the wall and add 7 inches —6 inches for casings, plus an additional inch for slack taken up when the rods are in the fabric. If you have a pattern repeat, add its length to the height measurement. Multiply this figure by the number of panels and convert to yardage measurement to arrive at the amount of fabric you need.

STITCHING & INSTALLING THE FABRIC

Cut the panels of fabric to the required length, matching patterns, if necessary. With right sides together, pin the panels. Using ½-inch seam allowances, stitch from the top edge to the bottom, backstitching at both ends. Fold the side edges under ½ inch and press; fold under ½ inch again and stitch close to the inside fold. Press the seams open.

(Continued on next page)

SHOP TALK

Using bed sheets for fabric walls can provide savings in time and money. Use these flat sheet finished dimensions to determine the size and number of sheets you'll need.

TWIN:	**66 x 96"**
DOUBLE:	**81 x 96"**
QUEEN:	**90 x 102"**
KING:	**108 x 102"**

To stitch casings and hems in the top and bottom edges of the fabric, press them under ½ inch; then

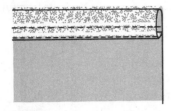

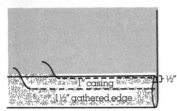

1" casing
1½" gathered edge
½"

press under 2½ inches. Pin and stitch close to the inside fold. Stitch again 1 inch from the first stitching line as shown. Iron creases out of fabric.

Attach the brackets for the rods to the wall; install the lower brackets upside down so the rod will be held securely.

Insert the rods through the fabric casings and gather the fabric evenly. Place the rods in the brackets, adjusting the gathers.

To reach outlets or switches, cut a slit in the fabric, turn the edges to the wrong side, and whipstitch in place.

When it's time to clean the fabric, simply remove it from the rods.

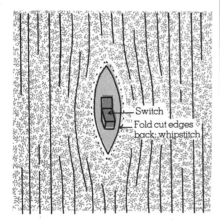

Switch
Fold cut edges back; whipstitch

COPING WITH OPENINGS

If the walls you're covering have window or door openings, you'll need extra rods and brackets to hang above and below the openings. The rods should equal the width of the opening.

Hang the fabric wall and adjust the gathers as described. Cut the fabric away from the opening, leaving an extra ½ inch on each side and 3 inches at the top and bottom. Remove the fabric from the rods and stitch new casings and hems to fit around the openings. Insert the rods, attach the new brackets, and hang the rods on the brackets.

PASTING FABRIC ON WALLS & CEILINGS

Pasting fabric to a wall differs from most other wall covering techniques in that the paste is applied to the wall, not the wall covering. The advantages of pasted walls are threefold: you can wash the fabric while it's on the wall; the fabric is resistant to steam; and you can easily remove the fabric without damaging the wall.

Before you decide to paste fabric to the walls, consider some drawbacks: this application reveals any imperfections on your walls and requires that colored walls be given a coat of primer so light-colored fabrics won't appear tinted.

Choose your fabric carefully. Light-colored fabrics with allover patterns work best. Fabrics with nap or porosity, such as velvet and wool, are not suitable for pasting. Nor are dark-colored fabrics: their trimmed edges can reveal white threads not penetrated by fabric dye, paste can stain the fabric, dark fabric dyes can bleed onto the wall, and seams will be distractingly obvious.

EQUIPMENT & SUPPLIES

Essential are a **plumb line, paint roller, razor knife, utility razor blades,** and a **broad knife** or straightedge.

You'll also need **vinyl wall-paper paste,** a large **sponge,** a **paint tray** for the paste, and several **drop cloths** to cover the floor. **Fabric shears** and ¾-inch push pins complete the list of supplies.

PREPARATION

To measure the area to be covered and determine the amount of fabric you'll need, see page 37. If you're covering the ceiling also, note the measuring instructions on page 63. Decide on the type of seam you'll use (see page 45) and allow extra width, if needed. We recommend butted edges because they're easier to use when matching a pattern, and with fabric, the seams won't shrink away when dry.

Measure and cut the panels according to the directions on page 56, with two differences: instead of adding 6 inches to the length for insurance, cut the ceiling edge of the fabric 2 inches above where you want the pattern to appear along the ceiling line; also, cut the bottom edge of the panel 2 inches below the baseboard edge.

Working on a hard, flat surface, cut the selvages from the fabric, using a razor knife with a sharp blade and holding a broad knife against the fabric to prevent razor mishaps.

Clean the walls thoroughly and allow them to dry. If the walls are a dark color, apply primer (see page 72). Put a small amount of paste in the paint tray; add enough water to thin the paste to about the consistency of cream soup.

PASTING THE FIRST STRIP

If you're planning to paste fabric on the ceiling as well as the walls, complete the ceiling work first. You'll find directions on the facing page.

Establish plumb (see page 42) and align the pattern along the ceiling line; remember to leave a 2-inch overlap. Tack the fabric along the ceiling line with push pins. Check to make sure the fabric is even with the plumb line and adjust, if necessary.

Lift the fabric out of the way and tack it to one side. Using a paint roller or brush, apply paste to the wall, starting at the ceiling line and pasting down a few feet and covering an area a few inches wider than the width of the fabric.

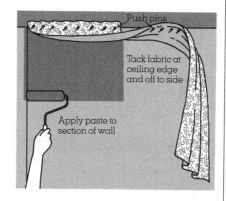

Remove the pins from the side-draped fabric, but not from the ceiling line. With your hands, lightly smooth the fabric into place. Work from the center out to the sides, being careful not to stretch the fabric. Make sure the edges are firmly in place. Paste down any loose threads or cut them with sharp shears; don't try to pull threads.

To eliminate bubbles, brush a small amount of paste on the fabric until it lies flat; to eliminate wrinkles, brush paste on the fabric and use your fingernail to smooth them out. Be sure to wipe off the surface with a damp sponge before the paste dries.

Tack the remaining fabric to the side and apply paste a few more feet down the wall. Repeat the procedure outlined above until the strip is completely pasted. Wipe excess paste from the surface with a damp sponge. Moisten the fabric overlaps at the ceiling and baseboard edges with paste. When dry, they'll be easy to cut off with a razor knife.

PASTING THE REMAINING PANELS

Hang each remaining panel using the seam you've chosen—butted, lapped or double cut (see page 45).

Following the instructions for pasting the first panel (preceding), paste the remaining fabric panels. To work around corners, openings, and fixtures, use the wallpaper techniques on pages 48–49.

If you must leave your project overnight, store paste and brushes as described in "Shop Talk" on page 44.

FINISHING

When the fabric has dried (at least 24 hours), use a razor knife to trim the overlapping fabric along the ceiling and baseboard; protect the fabric with a broad knife or metal straightedge.

If the razor edge slips while you're cutting, repaste the area and pat a matching fabric patch in place. When the paste dries, cut off any loose threads, and the patch won't be visible. You can also use this technique later, in the event of stains or damage.

Border fabric can be pasted on top of fabric walls after the wall is completely dry. Use the same procedure as for pasting walls, but make sure not to drip paste onto the fabric.

PASTING FABRIC ON A CEILING

If you want to paste fabric to your ceiling, do it before you begin on the walls. Measure as you would for walls, determining the length versus the width of the ceiling by the direction you want the fabric pattern to run.

Using heavy masking tape, secure the fabric to the ceiling in several places, letting the fabric hang loosely as shown above right.

Roll paste onto the area of the ceiling above the hanging fabric, covering no more than 2 feet lengthwise, but a few inches more than the width of the fabric. Remove the first set of tape strips and smooth the fabric into place as shown above right. Repeat until the fabric panel is

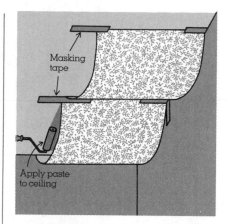

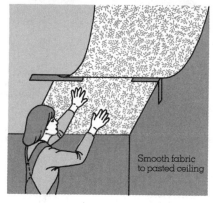

completely pasted. Follow the same procedure for the remaining fabric panels. Make seams and finish edges as for walls.

REMOVING FABRIC

Because the fabric is easy to remove, pasting fabric to walls is an apartment dweller's delight. Starting from a corner along the baseboard, gently peel the fabric from the wall as shown. The paste will come off with the fabric without damaging the wall surface. Using a damp sponge, wash the wall to remove any paste residue.

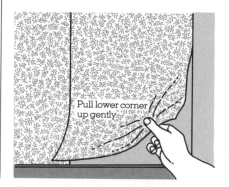

PAINT
A MASTER OF COLORFUL TRANSFORMATION

Paint—from the plainest whitewash on primitive walls to the most modern fashion color mix—has been, and probably still is, the world's most popular wall coating. Why? Because it's economical, easy to maintain, and the fastest and simplest way to transform the visual impact of a room or an entire house.

New paints feature the advantages of easier application, faster cleanup, and—most important—greater durability. The versatility of today's painting tools makes the job easy even for first-time painters.

This chapter will direct you in paint selection and introduce you to the awesome variety of paints and tools at your disposal. Also within these pages are instructions for surface preparation—essential for a durable wall coating—and the painting sequence you'll want to follow. Here, too, are hints for cleanup when the job is done.

If painting the four walls and ceiling of a room seems a bit overwhelming, you can get a real decorating boost by painting only one wall—choose a color that complements the color of the other walls and ceiling. And don't overlook the powerful new uses of paint in creating graphics, murals, and stenciled designs.

The following chapter focuses on interior painting, but a special section at the end treats exterior painting.

CHOOSING THE RIGHT PAINT

A would-be painter venturing into the world of paint must grapple with a confusing array of names and terms. This section defines the types of paint that are available and explains their use.

The profusion of brand names and grades makes selecting a quality paint even more difficult. One solution is to look for the more expensive brands. Though it may cost nearly twice as much as the cheapest paint, good quality paint covers in fewer coats and may require less frequent repainting.

But don't choose a paint by price alone. Your best bet is to consult a reputable paint dealer. You'll find most dealers to be quite knowledgeable about the quality of the various products, as well as the latest developments in both paint and equipment.

Each paint family has a different quality and a specific use. Paints for interior walls include water-base (latex) paints and oil-base paints. In addition, wood stains and clear finishes—polyurethane, varnish, and shellac—are available for use on wood. The last category of wall coatings in this section deals with paints for special situations.

In some localities, air quality control standards limit the amount of solvent that can be used in paint products. In those areas, oil-base paints for walls and ceilings are simply not available. But because there are no acceptable substitutes for certain products, primers, exterior stains, and all clear coatings are currently exempt from these restrictions and can retain their oil-base formulas.

LATEX PAINTS

Latex, a water-base paint, is the most popular surface paint today, and for good reason. Because water is the solvent, latex paints, also called acrylic or vinyl paints, have many advantages: they dry quickly (usually in little more than an hour), they're relatively odor-free, and they wash off tools—and your hands—with soap and water. They're also nontoxic, smooth spreading, and can be applied to damp surfaces.

Latex paints are durable and washable, but only when applied to a properly prepared surface. Surface preparation is extremely important to the bonding of a latex paint. If the walls aren't clean and primed (see pages 70–72), latex paint can peel and crack in a disappointingly short time.

You can apply latex to nearly all surfaces except tile and acoustical ceilings and walls (see page 66).

Latex finishes range from flat to glossy, though glossy latex paint doesn't have as much shine as a comparable oil-base paint. Flat vinyl, a specially made latex, has a dull finish that's washable and alkali resistant. Masonry surfaces are covered best by flat vinyl.

For kitchens, play rooms, and other areas that receive hard wear, use a semigloss enamel. The more glossy the finish, the more durable and washable it will be.

OIL-BASE PAINTS

A true oil paint—one in which pigments are ground in oil, such as linseed—is slow drying, strong smelling, and requires a harsh and equally strong-smelling solvent, such as turpentine, for cleanup.

Because of these problems, the formulas for oil-base paints have been revised to include alkyds. These resins produce paints that are durable, practically odor-free, and faster drying than plain oil paint. Though most of these paints don't require thinning (stirring is usually sufficient), paint thinner is required for cleanup.

Oil-base paints containing alkyds are more washable and durable than latex paints, and generally level out better, drying free of brush marks. They also have "bite," a sticking quality not inherent in latex.

Available finishes are flat, satin, semigloss, or glossy (the higher the gloss, the smoother the finish and the greater the washability and durability). Use a semigloss or gloss enamel finish for areas most susceptible to dirt and wear—the kitchen and bathroom, for example, or for woodwork.

A special type of oil-base paint—interior-exterior, quick-drying enamel—has a brilliant, tilelike finish that's extremely durable. Also highly resistant to odor and dirt, it's an excellent choice for kitchen and bathroom cabinets and closet doors.

Synthetic enamel and other newly developed enamels all have excellent washability and color retention; they range in sheen from high to very low and are used in the same way as standard oil-base paints.

WOOD STAINS

Since most stains are made for a particular wood, effect, or condition, it's best to discuss the job with your paint dealer before choosing one. Stains are available with oil, water, or alcohol bases; the amount of pigment they have determines the transparency or translucency of the stain.

One interior stain is in such general use and is so easy to apply that it deserves mention—it's pigmented or dye-colored wiping stain. You brush it on, wait awhile, then wipe it off.

POLYURETHANE, VARNISH & SHELLAC

Though sometimes pigmented, polyurethane, varnish, and shellac are generally clear finishes used to cover bare or stained wood surfaces when you want the grain to show through.

Polyurethane

Apply these plastic coatings to cabinets and wood paneling where extreme durability and washability are required. Available in both clear and colored finishes, they're easy to use. Polyurethane interior satin finish is a popular choice because neither scuffing, water, nor grease will harm the surface.

One type of polyurethane—penetrating resin sealer—soaks into the wood, rather than coating the surface. Use this finish where you want to maintain the wood's texture.

You'll need paint thinner for thinning and cleanup.

Varnish

Resin-base coatings, varnishes have many of the same uses as polyurethanes. Finishes range from low sheen to satin sheen and semigloss to high gloss. Varnishes are extremely tough and resist marring, abrasion, and water stains.

Your paint dealer can recommend the type of varnish that's best for your job. Use paint thinner for thinning and cleanup.

Shellac

Because it allows the wood grain to show through, shellac can be used for finishing wood paneling, cabinets, doors, and trim. Shellac is made from an alcohol solution; its finish is glossy, and its color is either natural (amber) or clear (white). Shellac dries in about 30 minutes;

any brush marks that appear when it's first applied aren't visible when it's dry.

A disadvantage of shellac is that water causes white spots to appear on the finish. For this reason, shellac isn't recommended for use in kitchens, bathrooms, laundry rooms, and other areas exposed to moisture. Use shellac only over bare or stained wood—other coatings could be dissolved by its alcohol content.

Use shellac thinner grade alcohol for thinning and cleanup.

SPECIAL PAINTS

Surfaces such as acoustical ceilings and walls, nonporous surfaces like tile, and walls with imperfections require special paints.

Acoustical ceiling paint. Acoustical ceilings and walls lose some of their sound-deadening qualities when covered with ordinary paint. Acoustical ceiling paint is a porous flat paint that doesn't change the panels' acoustics. It comes in only a few colors and is usually applied with a sprayer or a special roller.

You can apply acoustical ceiling paint to simulated acoustical surfaces, perforated acoustical tile, and mineral tile. It dries quickly to a flat finish. Thinning is done with water; cleanup is with soap and warm water.

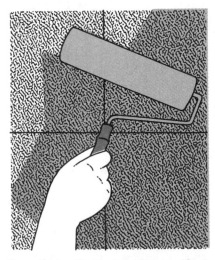

Acoustical ceiling paint rolls on easily; it doesn't change panels' acoustics.

The variety of paints and stains available for various kinds of surfaces is sometimes overwhelming. This chart will simplify the decision-making process.

Surface	Latex flat	Latex semigloss	Oil-base flat	Oil-base semigloss	Oil-base gloss enamel	Wood stain	Polyurethane	Varnish	Shellac
Gypsum board walls and ceilings	•	•	•	•	•				
Plaster walls and ceilings	•	•	•	•	•				
Wood paneling	•	•	•	•	•	•	•	•	•
Kitchen and bathroom walls	•			•	•				
Wood trim	•	•	•	•	•	•	•	•	•
Window sills	•				•		•	•	
Wood cabinets and shelves				•	•	•	•	•	•
Masonry	•								

Epoxy paint. For hard, nonporous surfaces (including ceramic and metal tile, plastics, porcelain, fiberglass, and glass), epoxy is the best—and sometimes the only—paint to use. It's usually found in a semigloss or high gloss finish.

Extremely durable, epoxy withstands scrubbing and resists abrasion. The most effective epoxies come in two cans that you mix together just before you begin the job. A disadvantage of epoxy is that it's so fast drying, it's difficult to apply without brush marks.

Textured paints. These include basic texture paint, sand paint, and stipple enamel. All are thick substances containing texturizers. They're popular because they both effectively disguise wall imperfections and have a pleasing effect.

You add a basic texture paint to a flat wall paint, then use a brush to apply it to a small area. While the paint is still wet, you create a rough finish with a trowel, putty knife, whisk broom, brush, sponge, paint roller, or other implement—even a piece of crumpled paper.

Sand paint is a latex to which you add 30-mesh sand or sandlike material. It produces a coarse finish, good for covering gypsum board's taped joints.

Stipple enamel also produces a textured effect—very much like the skin of an orange. It's available in various degrees of texture and in low and high gloss. Applied with a brush or roller first, stipple enamel is given its final texture with a carpet-type roller.

HOW MUCH PAINT WILL YOU NEED?

The spreading rate—the surface area a can of paint will cover—is marked on the paint label. You'll use this figure to help you calculate how much paint you'll need.

To determine the square footage of the area you plan to paint, measure the width of the surfaces and multiply the total by the room's height (for the ceiling, multiply the width by the length). Then estimate how much of this area contains surfaces that won't be painted, such as fireplaces, windows, and wall coverings, and areas you'll paint separately, such as woodwork. If these surfaces represent more than 10 percent of the room, deduct this amount from the total wall area.

Divide the square footage total by the spreading rate of the paint to determine how many cans of paint you'll need. For example, the square footage of a 16 by 20-foot room that's 8 feet tall is 576 square feet. If the paint's spreading rate is 400 feet per gallon, purchase two gallon-size cans. It's always better to have extra paint on hand for spills and for touchups later. Also, remember to double your total requirements if you're applying two coats.

SELECTING & USING TOOLS

Though choosing the right type and quality of paint is important, it alone can't guarantee a successful paint job. Even the best paint, if applied improperly and with the wrong tools, can produce disappointing results. If you choose your tools wisely and learn how to handle them correctly, you'll save yourself time and money.

TOOLS YOU'LL NEED

No matter how large or small the job, surface preparation and painting require the correct tools. Before you begin, carefully read the following section to make sure you have the necessary equipment (see illustrations on page 68).

Preparation tools

Proper wall preparation (see pages 69–72) is extremely important to the success of your painting project. Depending on the condition of your walls, you may need some or all of the following tools to make the necessary repairs: caulking gun and caulking compound, putty knife, hook blade scraper, wire brush, and paint scraper.

Brush choice is important

Choosing the correct brushes is almost as important as selecting the paint. The size of brush must be appropriate to the project and the type of bristle best suited to the paint you'll use. And you should be able to recognize the difference between good and poor-quality brushes.

Natural bristles (hog hair). Traditionally used to apply oil-base paints, polyurethane, varnishes, and shellac, natural bristles aren't suitable for applying latex paints; the bristles soak up the water in latex paints and quickly become soggy and useless.

Synthetic bristles. Though these nylon or nylonlike bristles are best for applying water-base paints, most can also be used with oil-base finishes. Soft-tip nylon brushes are suitable for applying varnishes and shellac.

What size brush? Having the right size brush can save you a lot of time

(Continued on page 69)

PAINTING TERMS YOU SHOULD KNOW

Acrylic. A resin used in latex paint to bind other ingredients.

Alkyd. A resin often used in oil-base paint.

Enamel. A finishing material with very fine pigment, providing a smooth, hard, semigloss or gloss finish.

Epoxy. An exceptionally durable, plasticlike paint used on nonporous surfaces.

Gloss. The degree of shininess of a paint finish. The higher the gloss, the more durable and longer lasting the finish. Paint finishes described as "glossy" have the highest luster; "semigloss" finishes have a medium luster; those described as "flat" have little luster.

Latex paint. A water-base paint, sometimes called vinyl or acrylic paint; cleanup is done with soap and warm water.

Oil-base paint. A paint made from oil, resins, and other ingredients; cleanup and thinning are done with paint thinner.

Polyurethane. A resin; also a common name applied to the plastic coating material made from this resin. Requires thinner for thinning and cleanup.

Primer. A first coat—usually a special paint—applied to help a finish coat adhere to the surface; may be made from a water-base or oil-base formula.

Shellac. A coating made from a resinous material called "lac" and used as a clear sealer or finish.

Thinners/solvents. Volatile liquids used to regulate the consistency of paint and other finishes; also used to dissolve oil-base paints for cleanup.

Varnish. A liquid coating that converts to a translucent or transparent solid film after application.

Vinyl. The name of a class of resins. Vinyl acetate is commonly used in latex paints. Polyvinyl chloride is used in some solvent-thinned coatings when high chemical resistance is necessary. Many other vinyl derivatives appear in various specialized coatings.

Water-base paint. See Latex paint.

Helpful Painting Tools

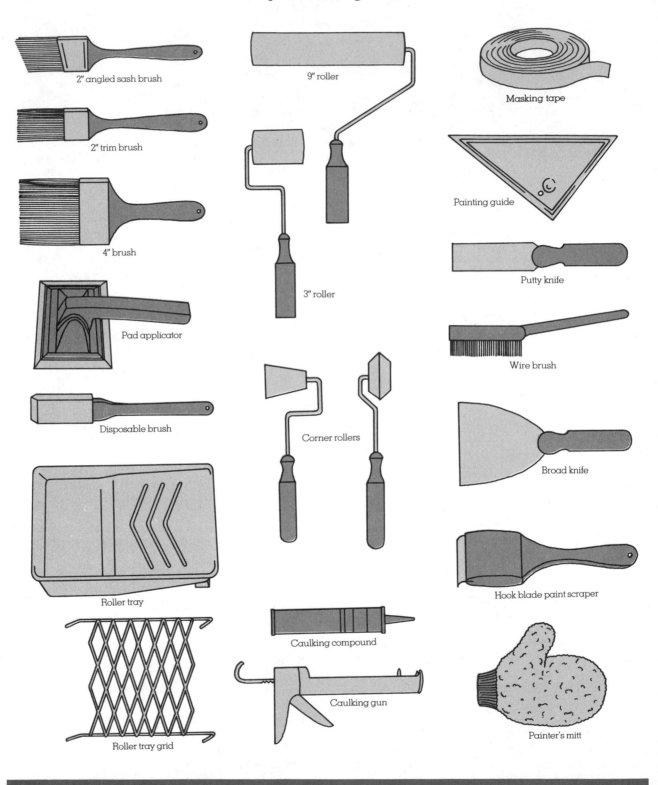

2" angled sash brush

2" trim brush

4" brush

Pad applicator

Disposable brush

Roller tray

Roller tray grid

9" roller

3" roller

Corner rollers

Caulking compound

Caulking gun

Masking tape

Painting guide

Putty knife

Wire brush

Broad knife

Hook blade paint scraper

Painter's mitt

and trouble. For painting trim and hard-to-reach places, a 1-inch brush does the job neatly. Window sashes, shutters, and trim are best painted with a 1½ or 2-inch angled sash brush.

For woodwork, cabinets, doors, cupboards, shelves, beams, stair steps, and other medium-size surfaces, use a 2 or 3-inch brush. For walls, ceilings, and most paneling, use a 3½ or 4-inch brush (you may prefer a roller for these large areas).

Checking for quality. Good quality brushes perform very differently from less expensive ones. To choose a quality brush, follow the guidelines below.

Check for "flagging" of the bristles (see below). "Flags" are the split ends of bristles, and you need lots of these—more flags mean more paint is held on the bristles permitting smoother application. Most of the bristles should be long, but check to make sure that some short bristles are mixed among the longer ones.

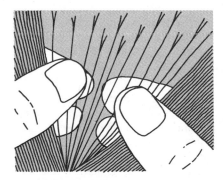

"Flagged" bristles varying in length are characteristic of quality brushes.

Bristles should be thick, flexible, and tapered so they're thicker at the base than at the tip. And they should be set firmly into the handle. A brush should feel comfortable in your hand—not so awkward or heavy that using it will tire you.

Paint rollers & trays

When you want to paint a large flat area quickly and easily, a roller is the answer.

Choosing a roller. A good roller has a heavy-gauge wire frame, an expandable cage-type sleeve, a cover, and a comfortable handle threaded to accommodate an extension pole. A 9-inch roller will handle nearly all interior paint jobs.

When you're choosing a roller, pay close attention to the roller cover. The nap material of the cover is either nylon blend, lambskin, or mohair. Nylon blend is recommended for use with latex, though it can be used with oil-base products. Lambskin covers are for applying oil-base paints only. A mohair cover provides the smoothest finish for both latex and oil-base paints.

Nap thickness varies from ¼ to 1¼ inches. Shorter napped covers are best for applying paint to smooth surfaces; medium-thick naps handle textured surfaces; long naps are necessary for rough surfaces.

For some jobs you may need these special rollers: a trim roller, 1 to 3 inches wide, for painting trim and window sashes; a corner roller with a beveled shape for corners, ceiling borders, and paneling grooves; a carpet roller for stippling (see page 66), and a roller made of grooved foam for acoustical surfaces.

A 3 or 4-foot extension pole allows you to reach high walls and ceilings, eliminating the need for ladders or scaffolding.

Roller trays. Roller trays—essential for roller painting—are available with either shallow or deep wells. Most have corrugated slopes to allow excess paint to be squeezed off the roller. A plastic or metal grid placed over the slope will help separate any residue of a thick paint.

Other tools for applying paint

In addition to brushes and rollers, you may want to consider these helpful paint applicators.

Pad applicators. Paint corners and edges easily with a pad applicator. It's faster to use than a medium-size brush and smoothes the paint more

evenly. Though its spreading rate is slower and its use requires some skill, a pad applicator is more versatile than a roller; it can reach into corners and fill in edges, and there's less drip. A pad applicator works well for painting trim, eaves, doors, and other areas with many edges.

Pad applicators have either a nylon, mohair, or lambswool applicator surface, a foam middle layer, and a rigid backing, all replaceable. You'll need the same accessories as for a roller.

Disposable applicators. A brushlike applicator that's disposable or has replaceable applicator pads is available. For small jobs or a quick touchup, a disposable spreader may be economical.

For difficult areas—a painter's mitt. A painter's mitt—a large, lambskin glove that fits over a plastic glove—is an old standby. With the mitt on your hand, you dip the glove into the paint. Very flexible, it's ideal for painting irregular surfaces such as pipes, grills, and radiators.

PREPARATION

Before you open even one can of paint, it's very important to prepare the area for painting. This may involve moving or covering furniture, preparing the surface and repairing any damages, and cleaning the surface so the paint will adhere.

ORGANIZING THE ROOM

Move all lightweight furniture and accessories into an adjoining room. If possible, push heavy furniture into the middle of the room and cover it with drop cloths.

Take down curtains and draperies (and all their fixtures, if you don't plan to paint them), along with all wall-mounted objects.

It's best to remove knobs, handles, and locks from doors, windows, and cabinets. Also, unscrew all switch and outlet faceplates.

To protect carpets or counters, use drop cloths. Plastic bags tied around immovable fixtures or objects you don't want to remove will protect them. To keep paint off window panes, line them with masking tape.

PREPARING THE SURFACE

Properly preparing the surface to be painted is a key factor in preventing cracking and peeling after the paint dries. It's *essential* to the bonding and durability of any latex paint application.

Stripping old paint

Sometimes the old finish is in such bad condition that the paint must be removed entirely. The easiest method of stripping old paint is to use a commercial liquid paint remover, though you may want to try an electric paint softener (see below). With either, the softened paint is scraped off with a broad knife or scraper. You'll then have to sand the surface lightly until it's clean and smooth.

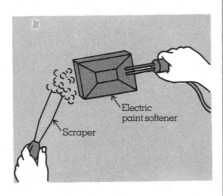

Electric paint softener

Scraper

Removing wallpaper

It's possible to paint over wallpaper, but it can be risky. The wallpaper must be smooth and stuck tightly to the wall for the paint job to be durable.

Inspect your wallpaper closely. If it's in good condition, remove or repaste any loose pieces and punc-

ture any air bubbles (see page 45). Then apply a sealing primer, such as pigmented shellac or flat oil-base enamel undercoat. Let the sealer dry completely before you paint.

It's best, though, to remove the wallpaper, especially if it's tearing and flaking (directions are on page 40). Make sure all the paste is removed and thoroughly wash the wall with an abrasive cleaner. Rinse well and allow the surface to dry for 24 hours.

Sandpapering

An old finish requires a light sanding if it's flaking lightly. Greasy areas on wood surfaces should be washed (see below) before sanding.

Rough bare wood needs sanding, as does a patched area. And when you plan to paint over a glossy paint surface, you must roughen the old finish so the new paint will adhere. On surfaces that have a very high sheen, start deglossing with a coarse sandpaper and finish with a fine-grit paper.

Dusting & washing

The last step of surface preparation is an overall dusting and thorough washing of the surfaces to be painted.

Begin by dusting everything. A good vacuuming is also recommended.

Wash the areas you plan to paint with an abrasive cleaner. Scrub a small area, rinse it well, and then move on. For excessively greasy spots, first use a sponge soaked with paint thinner. Blot the thinner dry and wash with the cleanser. Rinse the surface well.

Allow about 24 hours for all washed areas to dry completely.

REPAIRING HOLES & OTHER SURFACE DAMAGE

A new coat of paint may cover the surface at first, but if the surface hasn't been properly prepared, you'll be painting again in a short

time. Inspect the area you're painting for small holes, light flaking, and other minor damage not readily apparent, and make the necessary repairs.

Patching small holes & cracks

Fill nail holes with a tiny amount of wood putty or a ready-mixed spackling compound. Before patching small cracks and other small holes, brush them clean and dampen the surface (or better still, seal it with pigmented shellac and let it dry). Then fill the holes with wood putty, spackling compound, or patching plaster. Apply the filler with a flexible narrow-blade putty knife.

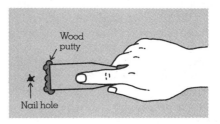

Wood putty

Nail hole

"Checking" describes a series of small cracks on wood surfaces (and in their finishes) caused by the expansion and contraction of the wood as it ages. Repairing these small cracks requires a little extra work.

Sand the damaged finish to bare wood. Apply a primer and allow it to dry thoroughly. Fill the wood cracks with wood putty, using a flexible knife. Apply a primer again and let it dry.

Sand all patched areas until they're smooth. If you're repainting with a light-colored paint, some patches may show through later; avoid this by priming the patches with the same color paint you'll be using for the finish coat.

Patching large holes & cracks

Repairs of this kind require a little extra time, care, and carpentry skill.

Holes in plaster over lath. Knock out all the loose plaster with a wire brush and an old screwdriver. Clean out the plaster in and behind the lath to provide a clean surface for the new plaster to adhere to. Brush the area clean and dampen it with a sponge for better adhesion; then force a layer of patching plaster between the lath strips.

If the hole is smaller than 4 inches square, fill it with one layer of patching compound; if larger, use three layers. The first layer should include some patching plaster that fills in behind the lath. Work from the outer edges to the middle as shown,

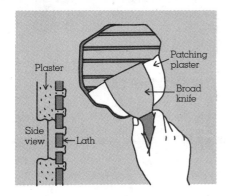

filling about one-third the depth of the patch. Score the first layer with a nail (see below) and let it dry.

Redampen the area and apply a second layer to two-thirds the depth of the patch. Allow it to dry; then finish filling the hole. When the surface is dry, sand it smooth and apply a primer or sealer.

Holes that have no backing. If the hole is 4 inches or less, clean it and cut a piece of wire screening slightly larger than the hole. Tie one end of a wire to the center of the screen; tie the other end to a 6-inch stick, as shown above right. Push the screen through

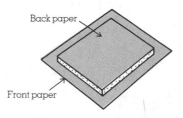

Wire screening

the hole, then draw the screen tightly to the back of the wall by rolling the wire up on the stick until the wire is taut (see below).

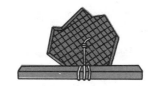

Dampen the area and fill the hole to half its thickness with patching plaster. Let the plaster dry thoroughly. Cut the wire even with the plaster and redampen the patch. Fill the hole flush with the wall. Allow it to dry; then sand it smooth and apply a primer or sealer.

Large holes in gypsum board. Using a sharp utility knife or hacksaw blade, cut a neat rectangle around the hole (see below). Then, from another piece of gypsum board, cut a patch 1 inch wider on all sides than the rectangle you've cut out of the wall.

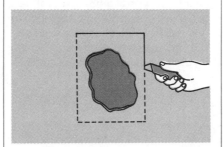

Laying the new piece of gypsum board surface side down, cut a plug the same size as the wall's rectangle

without scoring the paper on the surface of the gypsum board. Lift off the 1 inch of cut board around the sides of the patch from the front paper, leaving a 1-inch margin of paper around all four sides of the gypsum patch.

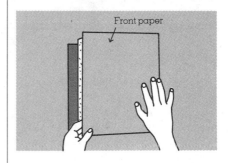

Back paper

Front paper

Spread a thin layer of spackling compound around and on the edges of the hole in the wall. Position the patch and press it into the hole until it's even with the wall surface. Cover

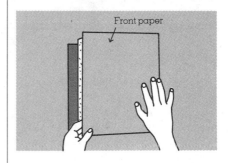

Front paper

the seams and entire surface with spackle; let it dry, then smooth it with sandpaper.

Large wall or ceiling cracks. Because of continuing structural expansion and contraction, cracks filled with rigid materials can give you continual trouble. The answer is a special crack patcher. A combination of a pliable coating material and an elastic bridging fabric, crack patcher "gives" with further house movements so cracks don't reappear. To apply, follow the manufacturer's instructions.

Repairing joint separations

Occasionally, an opening appears between different types of building materials, such as between a window frame and the wall surface. Minor gaps are easily sealed with caulking compound and a caulking gun.

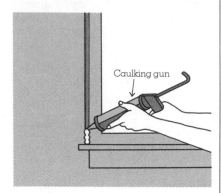

Caulking gun

For tips on repairing other separations, see the *Sunset* book *Basic Home Repairs.*

When the old paint gives out

Chalking, blistering, peeling, cracking, and flaking paint are all signs that the surface needs attention. Though common on exterior surfaces, these problems occasionally occur inside as well.

Chalking is the decomposition of a paint film into a loose powder that appears on the film's surface. Heavy chalking should be thoroughly brushed off before you repaint.

Blistering and peeling are normally the result of paint that was applied over a moist wood surface. If the surface is allowed to dry completely before painting, you probably won't have this problem.

But sometimes, moisture from a crack on the outside of the house or from a leaky pipe inside the wall seeps into the wood after painting, regardless of how careful you are. To remedy this, see "Water damage," at right.

Mildew also causes paint to blister and peel. For remedies, see page 41.

Cracking (or alligatoring) and flaking are the result of a mistake made in applying paint, perhaps applying the second coat before the first was dry, or applying too much paint.

Solve these problems by removing all loose paint. A hook blade

Paint scraper

scraper does a fast job on large areas; a broad knife is more convenient for small areas. A wire brush can handle any tiny flaking—use sandpaper to taper the edges. Sand all surfaces smooth and brush them clean. (If damage is excessive, remove all the paint; see page 70 for directions.)

Apply two coats of primer to repaired areas, allowing each coat to dry thoroughly. If you're not prepared to paint the entire wall surface, you'll have to apply one or more coats of the final finish to match the color and sheen of the old paint.

Water damage

Sometimes moisture penetrates a wall, flaking and staining paint and rotting wood.

First, get rid of the source of moisture. Cut out and replace any rotted wood. Then remove the old paint completely with a liquid paint remover or an electric paint softener (see page 70). Allow the surface to dry for several days; then apply a primer that has a pigmented, waterproofing sealer. As a finish, use a water-base paint; it will allow any undetected moisture to work its way out without flaking the surface.

PRIMING THE SURFACE

Most paints are designed to be used over some type of priming agent. The old finish, provided its condition is good, is usually all that's necessary. But in many cases, you'll need to use an undercoat. Here are the situations requiring a primer, followed by the particular primer to use:

• Unpainted wood to be finished with enamel or oil-base paint —use a flat oil-base enamel undercoat.

• Unpainted wood to be finished with latex paint—use an oil-base undercoat.

• Unpainted plaster or gypsum board—use latex paint or latex primer-sealer.

• Unpainted metal—apply a rust-inhibitive primer (each metal has its own particular primer).

• Rough, coarse, or porous masonry—use a block filler, a penetrating coating that fills holes.

• Dark-colored existing paint to be covered by a light-colored finish coat—apply an extra coat of desired color or a primer.

• Light-colored existing paint to be covered by a dark-colored finish coat—use two coats of dark-colored paint.

STIRRING THE PAINT

Most dealers will stir the paint for you when you buy it, especially if it's been custom colored. If the paint has been allowed to settle before application, though, it's best to stir it again just before you start painting, unless it's one of the newly developed paints that should not be stirred. Check the label first.

For paints that need stirring, begin by stirring up pigment that has settled at the bottom of the can. Continue stirring until there are no signs of color separation.

Never shake cans of varnish or polyurethane; if you do, you'll create bubbles that will last for 4 or 5 days.

THE PROPER PAINTING SEQUENCE

To avoid painting yourself into a corner, as well as splattering paint onto newly painted surfaces or inadvertently touching a just-painted edge, you'll want to follow the painting sequence outlined below.

Complete step-by-step painting instructions are on pages 73–75. Tips on painting trim, windows, doors, and cabinets follow.

PAINTING THE CEILING

If you're planning to paint the ceiling, begin there. Treat this as the big job it is—have a large roller and a 3 to 4-foot extension pole ready. Or create a simple scaffold by placing a plank between two ladders or between a sawhorse and a ladder.

To avoid painting over any edge that may have dried (this causes lap marks), paint the entire ceiling without stopping. Make sure the light is good enough so you can see how completely you're covering. And wear a hat—you'll quickly discover why hats are so popular among professional painters.

You'll want to paint in rectangles, approximately 2 by 3 foot, starting in a corner and working across the ceiling in the direction of the shortest distance.

Begin the first section by using a

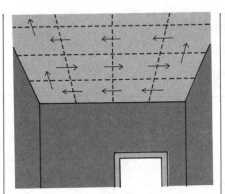

brush or corner roller to paint a narrow strip next to the wall line and around any fixtures. Then finish the section with a roller, overlapping any brush marks. Continue in the sequence shown in the drawing above.

PAINTING WALLS

Mentally divide the walls into 3-foot-square sections, starting from a corner at the ceiling line and working down the wall. As with ceilings, paint the edge of each section with a brush or corner roller along the ceiling line, corners, and fixtures or edges of openings. Finish each section with a roller or unloaded brush, overlapping any brush marks.

At the bottom edge along the

If the odor of paint bothers you, mix a few drops of vanilla or a commercial paint fragrance additive into the paint.

floor or baseboard, use a brush and paint guide, again overlapping edges with a roller. Return to the ceiling line and work down again in successive 3-foot-square sections as shown below.

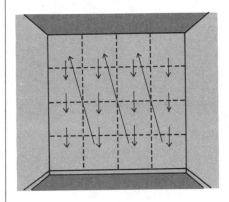

If you can't paint all the walls in one day, finish the wall you're working on before you stop so you can avoid having to paint over dry edges later.

SAFETY PRECAUTIONS YOU SHOULD KNOW

A few basic cautions before you start to paint:

• Be sure to check the labels on paint cans for warnings about possible hazards. Read all labels carefully—never ignore the instructions.

• Like other toxic materials, paints and paint products should be kept out of the reach of children.

• Always work with paint products in a well-ventilated area. Excessive inhalation of fumes from paints and solvents can cause dizziness, headaches, fatigue, and nausea. Also, keep pets out of freshly painted rooms; paint fumes are especially harmful to pet birds.

• Don't use or store paint products near a flame or

heat source. Avoid smoking while painting or using solvents. Store paint products in a metal cabinet.

• Many paints and solvents are particularly harmful to skin and eyes. Be especially careful when handling or applying products that contain strong solvents—again, read the labels. Wear gloves and a mask when necessary.

• Inspect ladders for sturdiness. Check scaffolding planks for splits, cracks, or other weak points. Never lean away from a ladder—get off and move it if you can't easily reach a particular spot.

• Clean up promptly after the job is finished, and properly dispose of soiled rags.

Painting with a Brush

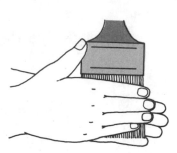

Step 1. Roll bristle ends between your palms to remove any loose bristles; shake brush vigorously. Moisten bristles thoroughly with appropriate solvent; wipe off excess.

Step 2. If paint requires stirring (check label), stir it thoroughly while it's still in can; pour into a clean rimless pail until pail is half-full. Dip brush half the length of its bristles into paint several times to saturate thoroughly.

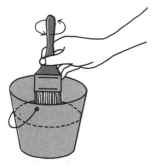

Step 3. Dip brush a third to half the length of its bristles into paint, gently stirring with brush to spread bristles slightly. (Don't stir on subsequent dippings.)

Step 4. Lift brush straight up, letting excess paint drip back into pail. Gently slap both sides of brush against inside of pail two or three times. Don't wipe brush across lip of pail, or bristles may separate into clumps, leaving less paint on brush.

Step 5. Work in approximately 3-foot-square areas. Spread paint with smooth, even strokes, gradually reducing pressure on brush as you approach end of each stroke. On smooth surfaces, direct final strokes one way. On rough surfaces, vary direction to help fill crevices. On wood surfaces, apply final strokes parallel to grain. Paint out to an edge, not in from it.

Step 6. Blend brush marks by running unloaded brush very lightly over wet paint. Begin next area a few inches away from last finished area. When new area is completed, brush into previously finished area, blending overlap.

Painting with a Roller

Step 1. Moisten roller cover with appropriate solvent, working it into nap. Blot with a cloth.

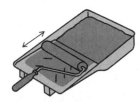

Step 2. Pour paint into roller tray until it's two-thirds full. Run roller back and forth in paint to soak it thoroughly. Pull roller up corrugated slope of tray.

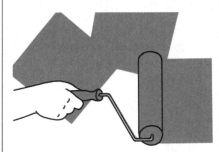

Step 3. Slowly roll paint onto surface with light, even strokes in all directions; roll as close to edges and corners as possible to cover any textural differences between brush and roller marks.

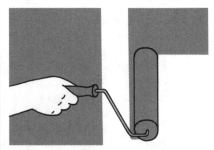

Step 4. Begin next area a few inches away from last finished area. Roll slightly into previously finished area, blending overlap. Finish by rolling unloaded roller in one direction.

Painting with a Pad Applicator

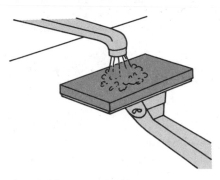

Step 1. Moisten pad with appropriate solvent, working solvent into foam backing. Blot with a cloth.

Step 2. Stir paint, if necessary, and fill roller tray (see "Painting with a Roller," Step 2, opposite). With edge of pad, draw paint up onto corrugated slope of tray. Rock applicator back and forth in paint on slope. (If using pan-type paint tray, dip only absorbent pad, flat side down, about ¼ inch into paint. Lift applicator straight up and let excess paint drip off.)

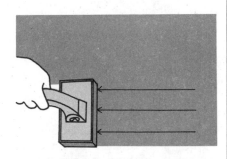

Step 3. To apply paint, use long, smooth pulling strokes in one direction. As you finish each stroke, tilt handle of applicator outward; this will produce a thin edge of paint for smooth blending with next stroke.

PAINTING THE TRIM

Painting trim is meticulous work that demands patience. For best results, use a 1½-inch angled sash brush to paint narrow molding and a 2-inch trim brush to paint wider trim (see page 68).

Begin with the trim closest to the ceiling and work down. Brush paint on smoothly and evenly, using a painting guide when you're next to another surface.

Save the baseboard for last. Using masking tape or a painting guide to cover the edge of the floor, paint the baseboard's top edge first and then the floor edge. To paint the

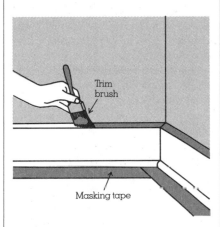

baseboard's vertical surface, use a wide brush.

PAINTING WINDOWS

The delicate business of painting windows has frustrated many a painter. In this section you'll find several tips for eliminating much of the difficulty.

A steady hand is the best tool for painting the wood parts of windows. Also important is the right brush—preferably an angled sash brush that reaches neatly into corners.

Resist the temptation to do a fast paint job, thinking you'll scrape off excess paint later; scraping can permanently scratch the window glass. Instead, cover the window edges with masking tape as shown above right.

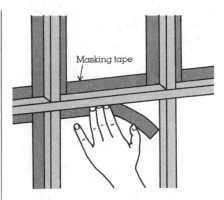

Double-hung windows. Raise and lower the sashes as needed to reach all the parts. Start with the outer (or

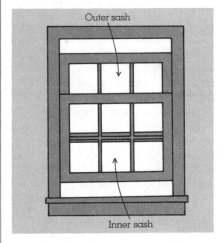

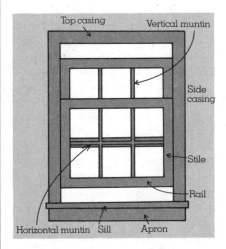

upper) sash. If your windows have small panes, start by painting the horizontal muntins (molding that divides the window into sections); then work on the vertical muntins. Next, paint the exposed parts of the stiles, and the top and bottom rails, in that order. Finally, paint the inner (or lower) sash, starting with the muntins and finishing with the rails.

To prevent sticking, carefully move the sashes once or twice while the paint is drying.

To paint the trim around a double-hung window, begin with the top casing and then paint down the sides. Next, paint the sill and finish with the apron.

If your windows are designed so the sashes can be removed, simply lift them out (weather conditions permitting), lay them on a table or other surface, and paint them. Be prepared to leave the sashes out long enough to dry thoroughly.

Finally, you need to wax the jamb (side lining where the window slides). Don't wax a metal jamb and don't paint any jamb—this can cause it to stick later.

Casement windows. First, paint any vertical muntins, then any horizontal muntins. Next, paint the top and bottom rails, and then the stiles. Then paint the casing as you would that of a double-hung window.

PAINTING DOORS

You can paint a door on or off the jamb—either way, the painting sequence is the same.

To remove a door, simply slip the hinge pins out, but never unscrew the hinges themselves. For painting, lean the door against a wall and place two small blocks of wood or rubber wedges under the bottom edge and a third wedge between the center of the top edge and the wall.

Or, you can lay the door across sawhorses. Working on a horizontal surface allows you to apply a good coat of paint without worrying about the paint collecting in the lower corners of the panels and eventually dripping down. But you do have to be careful not to apply too thick a coat or the paint may "puddle."

Standard procedure in painting doors is to move from top to bottom. For doors with inset panels, first paint the panel molding and the in-

side edges of the panel cavities. Next, paint the panels as shown.

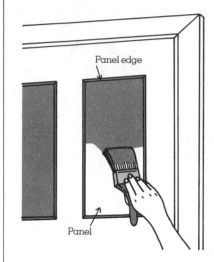

Panel edge

Panel

Then paint the horizontal and vertical strips around the panels. If the door opens into the room being painted, paint the door's latch edge. If not, paint the hinge edge. Don't close the door or rehang it until the paint has thoroughly dried.

For the door casing, begin with the top casing and work down the side casings. If the door opens into the room, paint the jamb and the door side of the door stop. If the door opens away from the room, paint the jamb and the two surfaces of the door stop (see illustration below). Keep the

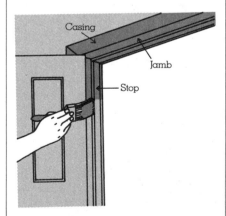

Casing

Jamb

Stop

door ajar until the paint on the jamb is completely dry.

PAINTING CABINETS

The following steps for painting cabinets will help prevent accidental

smears and spills. Using a brush with a shortened handle will also make it easier to paint small areas.

First, remove drawers and detachable shelves and place them on newspapers or drop cloths; paint them separately. Next, start inside the cabinet. Working from the top down, paint the back wall, the shelf bottoms, the side walls, and the shelf tops and edges, in that order.

Then, beginning at the top and working down, paint the outside surfaces of the cabinet.

Finally, paint the doors. Open them and paint the inside surfaces. Then push the doors nearly closed and paint the outside surfaces. *Caution:* Don't close the cabinet doors completely until the paint has dried.

CLEANING UP

Immediately after you finish using your tools, clean them. Don't wait—dry paint can make a later cleanup extremely difficult.

Cleaning brushes

To clean your brushes, follow the step-by-step process below as it applies to the type of paint you've been using.

For all brushes used in oil-base paint:

1) Remove excess paint from the brush with a scraper or by drawing the brush over a straight edge (not over the curved edge of a paint can).

2) Pour a small amount of thinner into a container. Protecting your hands with rubber gloves, force the thinner into the bristles—especially at the heel.

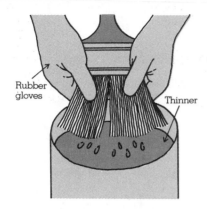

Rubber gloves

Thinner

3) When the thinner becomes saturated with paint, discard it and replace with new thinner.

4) Repeat steps 2 and 3 until the thinner remains clear.

5) To remove excess thinner, shake the brush vigorously or lightly tap the handle against a hard edge.

For synthetic brushes used in oil-base or latex paint:

6) Hold the brush under running water until the water runs clear.

7) Wash with soap and warm water, forcing water into the bristles and heel.

8) Rinse under warm running water.

For all brushes used in oil-base or latex paint:

9) Comb the bristles with a special comb made to keep bristles straight (see above right). Let the brush dry.

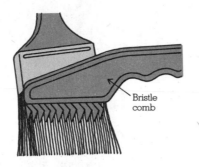

Bristle comb

10) Wrap the brush in its original covering or in stiff paper.

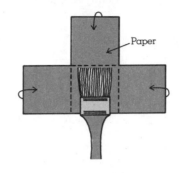

Paper

11) Store the brush by placing it on a flat surface or hanging it on a nail.

Cleaning rollers & applicators

To clean these painting tools, follow the steps below that apply to the kind of paint you've been using for your project.

For rollers and applicators used in oil-base or latex paint:

1) Remove the excess paint from your roller or applicator with the edge of a putty knife. You can also squeeze out paint by pressing the roller against the lip of the tray.

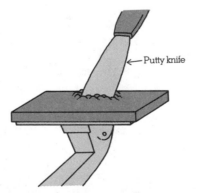

Putty knife

2) Remove the roller cover or spreader pad from its frame.

For rollers and applicators used in oil-base paint:

3) Pour thinner into a container. Protecting your hands with rubber gloves, wash the cover or pad thoroughly, forcing thinner into the nap.

4) Discard and replace the thinner when it becomes saturated with paint.

5) Repeat steps 3 and 4 until the thinner remains clear.

6) Squeeze thinner from the cover or pad; then wash the roller or spreader frame in the thinner.

For rollers and applicators used in oil-base or latex paint:

7) Hold the cover or pad under running water until the water runs clear.

8) Wash with soap and warm water, forcing water into the nap; then wash the frame.

9) Rinse the cover or pad and frame under warm running water.

10) Squeeze excess water out of cover or pad. Blot lightly with a clean, absorbent cloth and set aside to dry completely.

11) Wrap the cover or pad in a plastic bag or wrapping paper.

12) Store the roller cover on its end to prevent flattening the surface.

Cleanup & storage

With the appropriate solvent, clean your preparation and painting tools.

Most leftover paint can be stored in a tightly closed can for several months or more.

If less than a quarter of the paint in a can remains, transfer it to a container small enough to be almost filled (less air in the can means the paint has less chance of drying out); seal it tightly. Before covering a can of oil-base paint, pour a very thin layer of thinner on top of the paint.

Wipe off paint from the rim of the can to permit an airtight seal and to prevent paint from spattering when the lid is put on. Then firmly hammer the lid on the can.

(Continued on next page)

It's best to store all solvents and inflammable paints (check labels) in a metal cabinet. Keep paints and paint products out of the reach of children, and don't store such products near a flame.

Quick cleanup for yourself

Water-base paints come off easily with soap and warm water. Dried latex easily comes off your skin—but not your clothes. So wash your clothes before the paint has thoroughly dried.

Oil-base paint spots take a little more effort. For spots on arms and hands rub lightly with thinner, working quickly. On face and neck, dab the spots off with a cloth dipped in thinner. Be extremely careful to keep thinner *away* from your eyes. Then wash with soap and water, and apply a lotion to the cleaned areas.

PAINT AS ART

Special paint treatments such as graphics, murals, and stenciling can transform your walls into works of art and make them the focal point of the room. All you need is paint and a little imagination.

GRAPHICS

Used primarily to highlight architectural features or major furnishings, graphics are also good vehicles for adding a splash of color when you don't want to repaint an entire room. Depending on the effect you want to achieve, colors can be subtle shades of the wall color or vibrant, contrasting colors.

If the area you're planning to cover with a graphic design isn't newly painted, it must be properly cleaned and prepared (see pages 70–72) before you can begin.

Plan your graphic design to scale on graph paper. Then use a tape measure and chalk to transfer the design lines to the wall. If you want to reproduce the graph paper grid on the wall, snap chalk lines vertically and horizontally (for directions, see page 51). Then use chalk to mark the design within the grid lines.

Place masking tape along the outside edge of the design lines, one color section at a time. Use specially made paint masking tape—it won't lift any paint off the wall when it's removed. Be sure the tape is secure so paint can't seep under it. Let the paint set before removing the tape.

MURALS

Bring a whole new field of vision into your room with a mural.

One type of mural, the *tromp l'oeil*, is the master of deception. Literally meaning "fool the eye," tromp l'oeil is a technique that can produce a startlingly lifelike mural. It can enlarge your room dramatically by adding a garden that seemingly goes on forever, or a window with a beautiful "view" of the mountains.

It's the use of shading in the tromp l'oeil mural that suggests three dimensions, instead of two. Because of this feeling of depth, even a stylized rendition of an object will fool the viewer at first glance.

If you want the originality of a mural but aren't confident about your skills, consider a do-it-yourself mural kit, available at many paint stores.

Preparation for painting a mural is the same as for graphics. To plot your design and transfer it to the wall, see the instructions above.

STENCILING—A TRADITION FOR TODAY

Stenciling, a traditional form of wall decoration, is regaining some of its former popularity, even as it takes on some modern interpretations. It's an easy and inexpensive technique with powerful, exciting, and unique results.

Add a stencil design to the walls as a finishing touch to any room. The design can run vertically, horizontally, around corners, or even over the entire wall. You can pick up a pattern from draperies, upholstery, or bathroom tiles, or use your own design, highlighting the colors of a rug or favorite piece of art.

Supplies you'll need

Most of the tools and supplies you'll need can be purchased where artists' supplies are sold or ordered from paint manufacturers or stencil kit companies. Paints recommended for stenciling include japan, acrylic, and artists' oil paints. **Japan colors** (japan paints or signwriter's japan colors) are flat, opaque paints that dry instantly. You'll need turpentine for thinning and cleanup.

Acrylic paints are water-base paints, providing for easy cleanup and quick drying. Use them only with mylar stencils (see "Making a Stencil," facing page), since these paints can cause the edges of acetate to curl after repeated use.

Artists' oil paints provide brilliant colors, but take a long time to dry and require some skill to avoid smudges. Use them alone or mixed into japan colors to add brilliancy. Turpentine is the recommended solvent.

Stencil brushes have stiff bristles cut off bluntly at the end; they're arranged in a thick circular shape. You'll need a separate brush for each color.

Stencils may be purchased ready-made or in kits containing paints. For unique designs, you can make your own stencils (see "Making Your Own Stencil," facing page). To apply stencils, have on hand a **steel tape measure, plumb line, chalk, masking tape,** lots of **paper towels,** and a **drop cloth.**

Preparation & planning

Clean and paint the walls before you begin stenciling. To paint, use either a flat or satin-finish water-base or oil-base paint (see page 65). Glossy finishes aren't recommended because the stencil paints won't adhere to the surface. Wood surfaces can be painted, stained, or varnished; use either a satin or semigloss finish.

Next, check the walls, ceilings, and floors for straightness. If there's any curvature, you'll have to hang plumb lines (see page 42) to set a straight path for your stencils.

To plan placement, measure the width (or height for vertical placement) of the wall to determine how many stencil repeats will fit. Arrange designs from the center of the wall out to the edges so corners will match. You may want to reduce the space between designs so they'll be complete at the corners.

Make a colored print of your stencil on a piece of paper and hang it on the wall. Check it for size, scale, color, and placement. Using a steel tape measure or a chalk line, mark stencil placement guidelines.

Applying the paint

It's best to work with only a small amount of paint at a time. Since the paint is applied thinly, a little goes a

---

MAKING YOUR OWN STENCIL

The number of stencils you'll need for your design depends on how many colors you're using and how intricate your design is. Each color requires a separate stencil, unless the design cuts are spaced far apart. If the design has many small pieces or lines running closely together, use separate stencils.

Materials you'll need

Purchase either **clear acetate** (.0075 gauge) or **frosted mylar** (.005 gauge) for the stencil. Acetate, for use with japan or oil paints, is transparent, so you can layer as many pieces as you need when you're transferring the design and you'll still be able to see the original design clearly. Mylar is translucent; you'll only be able to layer up to four sheets on your design. You can use mylar with acrylic or japan paints.

To trace designs onto the stencil material, use a **technical drawing pen** and **India ink.** A black felt-tip pen also works on mylar.

You'll need a **utility knife, sharp razor blades,** and a piece of **plate glass** to cut the stencil. Cover the edges of the glass with masking tape.

Transferring the design

Draw the design to the desired size and color it. Be sure the drawing begins and ends at the same place so there's no break in the design when it's repeated.

Cut the stencil material to the size of the design, adding a 1-inch margin to all edges.

Tape the stencil material over the design and trace the design lines for the first color. If you're using more than one stencil, leave the first one in place and tape additional ones on top. Add registration marks to each one. To make a registration mark, trace an area of the design from the first stencil using a dotted line. Don't cut this line, but use it for aligning the new stencil with the pattern.

Mark the top right side of each stencil and number the stencils in their order of application.

Cutting the stencils

Place the stencils, one at a time, on the plate glass; be sure the glass is on a flat, firm surface. Using a utility knife, cut the stencil. Draw the knife towards you in a smooth, continuous movement. Trim any jagged edges.

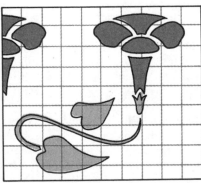

Design drawn on graph paper

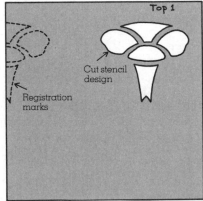

First sheet of acetate

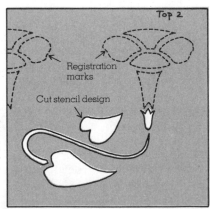

Second sheet of acetate

long way; also, stenciling paints dry quickly on your palette. Mix paints to a creamy, not runny consistency. If necessary, add a drop or two of thinner to japan and oil paints.

With masking tape, secure the first stencil to the wall along the guidelines. Dip the tip of the stencil

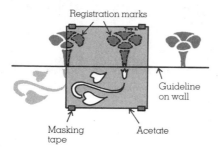

Registration marks

Masking tape

Acetate

Guideline on wall

brush into the paint, picking up only a small amount of paint. (If there's too much paint on the brush, paint can seep under the stencil edges.)

Apply paint either by pouncing the brush (tapping it directly against the wall) or by using a circular motion working from the outside of each shape toward the center. Though

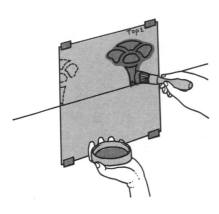

pouncing is the traditional method, it will make your arms sore quickly. Both methods will produce an attractive variation of color, but don't let the color become inconsistent or faded.

After you've filled in all the shapes on the stencil, leave the stencil on the wall for about a minute. Then remove it and continue to the next stencil placement.

Before the paint dries, wipe off smudges. Also keep some extra wall paint on hand for any spills.

Finishing up

When your project is completed, clean and store your tools (see page 77). Gently wipe the stencils with paper towels and solvent, keeping the stencils flat to prevent tears. Store them flat.

It's not necessary to apply a finish over the stenciled areas, unless you want extra protection. To protect against water and dirt, coat the stenciling with flat varnish (you'll get a slightly amber cast). After several months, stenciled walls can be cleaned with mild soap and warm water.

EXTERIOR PAINTING

Painting the exterior of a house differs somewhat from painting the interior. You'll need different paint, extra painting equipment, and some special techniques. You may also find exterior surfaces more difficult to prepare and paint because they're often weathered by sun, wind, rain, or snow.

WHEN SHOULD YOU PAINT?

The right time to repaint a house is just before it needs painting—not after.

If you repaint too often, you'll end up with a too-thick coating that's brittle. It will be subject to cracking and flaking because it won't be able to adjust to structural movements of the house. On the other hand, if you allow the paint to deteriorate too badly, you'll find it harder to restore the surface to a good appearance.

Signs of a surface worn badly enough to warrant repainting include these: the wood grain becomes more pronounced, the primer shows through, and the color fades.

SELECTING THE RIGHT PAINT

The guidelines below will help you select the best paint for the job. Be-

fore making a final decision, though, consult your paint dealer. Also, check the label on the paint can for possible warnings about painting in low or extremely high temperature and humidity levels—this advice can make or break a paint job.

Exterior latex paints. These paints have the same qualities as interior latex paints (see page 65). Latex is recommended for all exterior wood, masonry, stucco, concrete, and cinder block surfaces. It's also suitable for galvanized metal and cement-asbestos boards.

Two special outdoor latex paints are available for certain situations: use exterior latex trim enamel on exterior trim, doors, and woodwork; apply latex masonry paint to brick, stucco, concrete, and cinder block.

Exterior oil-base paints. These are the preferred finishes for exterior surfaces where durability and gloss are required.

• Use exterior oil-base enamels on all properly primed wood surfaces, such as siding, sashes, trim, shutters, and doors, and metal surfaces like gutters, rails, and steel sashes.

• Exterior flat finish is recommended primarily for rough siding, board and batten, and cedar shingles and shakes. It can also be used on other properly primed surfaces and may be thinned enough for use as a heavy-bodied stain (but a prepared stain will do a better job).

• Porch-and-deck paints are available for use on both concrete and wood surfaces. If the concrete surface is glossy, roughen it with muriatic acid before applying the paint so the new paint will adhere. Apply a primer to wood surfaces before using porch-and-deck paints.

Spar varnishes. Tougher than interior varnishes, spar varnishes are recommended for such exterior surfaces as doors, sashes, trim, and siding.

Penetrating wood stains. These semitransparent stains highlight the grain and texture of wood, and are available in both oil-base and water-base types.

Solid color stains. Thick enough to produce a nearly opaque finish, these stains are available in both oil-base and water-base types.

Cement powder paint. This is a popular, low-cost finish for unpainted masonry and other unpainted rough surfaces, including brick, block, stucco, and concrete. It's a powder composed of white Portland cement, pigments, and a small amount of water repellent. Before application, you add water to get the right consistency.

TOOLS & SUPPLIES

In addition to the brushes and rollers recommended for interior painting, you may need larger applicators for exterior surfaces. Block brushes—ranging from 4 to 6 inches wide—will help you cover large flat surfaces quickly. A big, thick-napped roller is another time-saving tool. Also available are large applicator pads that can be attached to standard-size pad applicator frames.

Consider using a compressed-air spray painting system for large areas. It's a fast technique for painting the exterior of your house. Also ask about the "airless" spray unit. It produces a direct spray of pure paint without any overspray.

An extension ladder is a must for exterior painting, particularly for two-story homes. For stability, place the ladder on firm, level ground at a distance from the house equal to a quarter of the vertical distance from the ground to the top rung.

If the paint is badly worn, make surface preparation easier by using large scrapers, wire brushes, and an electric sander. For other repairs, you may need window sash putty, stucco or masonry patching compound, and a little carpentry skill.

PREPARING THE SURFACE

As with interior painting, the most important part of exterior painting is surface preparation. Here's a check list of things you may need to do:

1) Remove outdoor light fixtures, hardware, screens, shutters, and house numbers for separate painting.

2) Repair any structural damage (see the *Sunset* book *Basic Home Repairs*).

3) Repair peeling, flaking, and mildew damage and remedy their causes (see pages 70–72).

4) Reset or replace popped-out nails.

5) Roughen high gloss areas so the finish coat will adhere better.

6) Cover bare wood surfaces with a primer.

7) Seal open joints around windows and trim with caulking compound.

8) Hose off dirt and excessive chalking of old paint.

9) Replace any loose or missing window putty.

10) Pull plants away from walls with rope or heavy twine and cover them with drop cloths.

11) Place drop cloths where necessary to protect patios, porches, and other floor surfaces.

WHERE TO START PAINTING?

Because the color of the paint can change dramatically when exposed

to the elements over a period of time, it's important to finish painting the exterior of your house in one season.

It's best to begin at the top of the house and work down, applying paint to areas within comfortable reaching distance as you stand on the ladder. Start with gutters, top portions of downspouts, eaves, peaks, gables, or porch ceilings. (Use rust-resistant paint for the inside of gutters.) Don't apply paint too thickly to surfaces protected from the elements. Little wear occurs in these places, and an overly thick coating will quickly crack and peel.

Still working from the top down, paint the house walls as you would interior walls (see illustration on page 73). On horizontal wood siding, apply paint to the bottom edges of two or three boards (see below); then

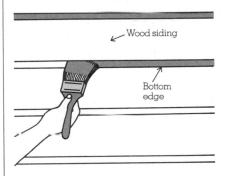

Wood siding

Bottom edge

smooth out the paint on the flat surfaces as shown. Force paint into rough surfaces, such as shingles and shakes, to fill the crevices.

As you work down the ladder, leave a very lightly painted edge along areas you've finished. After you've moved the ladder and are painting another top-to-bottom strip, you'll paint over these light edges and not create a heavy overlap.

Paint the trim, windows, and doors, following the interior painting procedures (see page 75).

Porches, patios, and steps are next (remember to leave one access to the house unpainted while the others are drying). Don't forget metal railings and other accessories.

Finally, paint the items you removed from the house and replace them after they've dried completely.

PANELING
UNPARALLELED TEXTURE & WARMTH

Picture sitting by the fire on a quiet evening, or curling up in a cozy study with a good book, or gathering friends together for a festive dinner party, and you'll probably envision the texture and warmth of a paneled room. Wood, whether in the form of solid board or sheet paneling, adapts to any setting. You can choose from among many species, each of which has its own character. Some are perfect for casual, rugged appearances; others enhance the elegance of formal rooms.

Whatever type you choose, wood paneling is durable and easy to maintain; moreover, it can conceal problem walls that would be very difficult or costly to repair. For a good product that will last many years without replacement, a wood wall covering is an investment worth considering.

We begin this chapter with descriptions of the various types of wood paneling. Instructions on how to prepare walls, how to install the paneling, and how to add moldings for the finishing touch follow.

To add another element of design to your paneled walls, you can attach solid board paneling in a particular pattern, such as herringbone, board on board, or diagonal. Instructions are given for a number of different applications.

No matter what type of installation you choose, you'll find that with some simple carpentry tools you can transform an existing room into an exciting new environment.

SOLID BOARD & SHEET PANELING

Paneling a room, or even just a wall, is a dramatic way to improve the appearance and feel of a room—and it doesn't require any special skills.

The two main types of paneling are board paneling and sheet paneling. The board paneling category encompasses the various species and millings of solid wood. Within the sheet paneling group are plywood, hardboard, and a few other less frequently used materials.

You'll find that board paneling is easier to use where extensive handling, maneuvering, and cutting are needed, such as around doors and windows. On the other hand, sheet paneling is easier to apply over large, unbroken surfaces because of its large dimensions.

SOLID BOARD PANELING

Because of texture, subtle variations in color and grain, imperfections, and natural fragrance, solid board paneling is particularly warm and inviting.

Solid board paneling is, simply, paneling made of solid boards. In some cases, it's regular lumber— 1 by 4s, 1 by 6s, and so forth. But most of the time, the boards used have edges milled to overlap or interlock. The three primary millings—square edge, tongue-and-groove, and shiplap—are shown below.

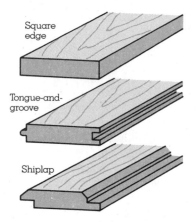

Square edge

Tongue-and-groove

Shiplap

Thickness of paneling boards ranges from ⅜ inch to ⅞ inch. The most common thicknesses, though, are ½ inch and ¾ inch.

Board widths range from 3 to 12 inches; but remember that these are nominal—not actual—sizes. A 1 by 4 is not 1 inch by 4 inches. Drying, surfacing, and milling the edges reduce the size to about ¾ inch by 3½ inches (the actual width depends upon the milling). See "Shop Talk" (at right) for the actual size of lumber.

Standard lengths are 8, 10, 12, 14, and 16 feet.

No matter what the milling, boards may be rough or smooth. The grade of wood may be "clear" for a smooth, formal appearance or "knotty" for a rough, informal appearance.

Solid board species

Hardwood boards are milled from broad-leafed, deciduous trees such as birch, cherry, mahogany, maple, oak, pecan, rosewood, teak, and walnut. The **softwoods** come from evergreens (conifers)—cedar, cypress, fir, hemlock, pine, redwood, and spruce.

Barnwood, a softwood like redwood or cedar, is a popular choice. One type is simulated; another is actually weathered, aged boards that have been salvaged from old, un-

painted barns and shacks. Few lumberyards stock authentic barnwood because it's difficult to find, somewhat fragile to handle, and not uniform in size.

A **simulated wood surface** is sometimes applied to a wood fiber core to produce a less expensive board paneling. The most common thickness is ¼ inch.

A word about cost

Prices for solid boards vary with availability. For example, redwood is considerably cheaper in some western areas than it is on the east coast. Generally, solid board paneling is more expensive than sheet paneling. This is particularly true of hardwoods and defect-free ("clear") softwoods.

To keep costs down, choose a species or pattern that's stocked locally. Extras such as transportation charges and special milling can run quite high.

Installation patterns

Solid board paneling has come a long way from the days when it was almost always installed vertically. Now, many different patterns have become popular, including horizontal, diagonal, herringbone, random width and thickness, board and batten, board on gap, board on board, and strip-facing patterns (for some examples, see "Patterns for solid board paneling," pages 93–95).

Instructions for installing boards in these patterns, as well as the necessary preparatory steps, begin on page 85.

SHEET PANELING

Sheet paneling is a catchall term for wall paneling that comes in large panels—most commonly 4 by 8 feet. Detailed instructions for installing sheet paneling begin on page 90.

All sheet paneling products are machine made. The two main types are created either from thin layers ("veneers") of wood that are sand-

wiched and glued together, or from compressed wood fibers and other recycled wood particles. The sandwiched type is plywood; the compressed panels are hardboard.

But when you look at a wall panel, you don't see plywood or hardboard. What you see is the panel's surface veneer, treated by the manufacturer in any of a variety of ways. Some surfaces are meant to be painted, some resemble real wood, and others are veneered with real wood that's either prefinished or meant to be finished by the buyer.

Sheets of gypsum board provide a surface smooth enough to apply any type of wall covering over them, from paint to paneling. Or purchase gypsum board factory decorated.

Plywood

The better plywood sheet panels have surface veneers of real wood —in an astounding variety. You can buy just about any species of hardwood and most of the major softwoods laminated onto the surfaces of plywood panels. Less expensive than solid boards, plywood panels won't warp.

Plywood comes in textures ranging from highly polished to roughly textured. The wood veneers are real to the touch, and many have the warm fragrance of wood.

Standard plywood sheets are 4 by 8 feet, but you can get some types in 4 by 9 or 4 by 10-foot dimensions. The standard thickness of interior sheet paneling is ¼ inch; avoid thinner panels—they're difficult to work with and not very durable. Exterior plywood sidings—ideal choices where you want rustic, rough-sawn textures—come primarily in two thicknesses: ⅜ inch and ⅝ inch. The ⅜-inch thickness is ample for interiors.

Hardboard

Hardboard is tough, pliable, and water-resistant. It's sold in 4 by 8-foot sheets that range in thickness from ³⁄₁₆ to ⅜ inch, though ¼ inch is standard.

The most common surface finishes are imitation wood; generally, these are grooved to look like board paneling. Wood imitations are available in highly polished, rough-sawn, or hand-hewn textures.

In addition to the wood finishes, you can find panels embossed with a pattern—basket weave, wicker, or louvered, to name a few.

Generally, the more expensive panels look convincingly like the materials they imitate. Inexpensive panels are likely to have less convincing enameled finishes or thin outer surfaces or photo-printed vinyl.

Hardboard with a vinyl or plastic-laminated finish that's easily cleaned and sheds water is available for installation around tubs and showers. The plastic-laminated type is the most durable. Tub and shower enclosures also come in kit form,
packaged with the necessary hardware and instructions for easy installation.

One familiar type of hardboard—pegboard—has a regular pattern of holes drilled in it for use with hardware hangers. You can use pegboard very effectively as a storage wall.

Gypsum board

A very popular paneling material, gypsum board is used as both a finish material and a backing for other paneling materials. The two main kinds available are a standard type that serves either as a complete, finished wall or as backing board, and a factory-decorated variety to use as a finished wall.

Panels are 4 feet wide and range in length from 8 to 16 feet. They're available in thicknesses from ⅜ to ⅝ inch.

PANELING TERMS YOU SHOULD KNOW

Backing board. Material, often gypsum board, fastened to wall studs to give paneling rigidity, offer sound insulation, and provide fire resistance.

Batten. Small-dimensioned board (often 1 by 2) generally used over seams of wide boards.

Blocking. Short lengths of 2 by 4s installed horizontally between studs to provide a nailing base for paneling.

Chalk line. Line used for marking a straight line across a distance (see page 51).

Countersinking. Using a nailset to drive nails so their heads are slightly below the surface.

Furring. Strips of wood evenly spaced and nailed to a wall to provide a flat and plumb surface for paneling.

Miter box. A tool used for guiding a handsaw to cut angles accurately.

Miter joint. Two pieces of material (usually molding) cut at an angle so their edges fit together without showing end grain.

Molding. Strips used for finishing and decorating. In paneling, molding can be used where paneling meets ceiling, floor, and openings, and as decoration on walls.

Nominal lumber dimensions. Sizes used when buying lumber. Actual sizes are smaller.

Plates, top and bottom. Horizontal 2 by 4s to which studs are attached, framing walls in a house.

Scoring. Marking with a sharp tool.

Scribing. Duplicating a wall's uneven contour on the surface of a panel.

Shimming. Filling out an uneven space by inserting pieces of tapered wood, often shingles.

Template. A pattern used as a guide to cut shapes accurately.

Wainscot. A facing, usually wood, used on the lower part of a wall. Wall area above is finished in a different material; molding often separates the two treatments.

Other sheet paneling materials

Each of the following unusual and somewhat specialized paneling materials fills a specific need. Though not designed as wall paneling, these materials can be used for that purpose under the right circumstances. For information and installation techniques, consult your dealer.

Particle board (chipboard). Made from particles of wood impregnated with glue and compressed into 4 by 8-foot sheets, particle board is quite heavy and the least expensive sheet material sold.

Unfinished panels have a speckled appearance and come in thicknesses of ½, ⅝, ¾, and 1 inch. Until recently, particle board was seldom used in paneling. But its recent use in finished furniture has stimulated experimentation. In some areas, prefinished particle board covered with simulated wood finishes is available.

Very heavy in weight, particle board must be glued or bolted to the wall. Water-base paints aren't recommended for finishing, since they soak into the panels.

Fiberboard. With very little effort, you can poke a hole in fiberboard; it's not known for its durability and ruggedness. Though it's an unlikely candidate for such heavy action areas as family rooms, children's rooms, or hallways, fiberboard can be an inexpensive, sound-absorbing choice above wainscoting and in dens, libraries, or other areas of restrained activity.

Acoustical board. Like fiberboard, acoustical board is not durable. But it has better sound-absorbing qualities than fiberboard.

Panels are 1 inch thick, 2 to 4 feet wide, and available in lengths from 6 to 12 feet. Acoustical material also comes in "tiles" of various sizes, lock-jointed for easy installation. Typically, a tile has small holes in regular or decorative patterns on the surface. It comes with a flange for stapling to furring or with a beveled edge for application with adhesive.

ORGANIZING YOUR MATERIALS

Once you've decided on the kind of paneling you want to install—and the pattern—some preliminary steps remain before you climb into your working clothes.

You'll need to measure the wall or room to be paneled, estimate the amount of paneling you'll need, buy the paneling, gather the necessary tools and equipment (see illustration on page 87), and even condition certain types of paneling before installation.

ESTIMATING & BUYING MATERIALS

For board paneling or for complex installations, the job of estimating materials takes some effort. To begin, use a steel tape to measure the wall or walls you plan to panel. Using graph paper, make a scale drawing of the area and transfer the figures to the drawing. Add any windows, doors, or other large openings and note their dimensions.

Figure the total wall area by multiplying its height by its width. From this amount, subtract the area of all openings.

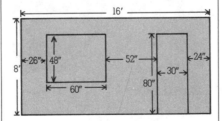

Then, decide on the pattern of application (see pages 93–95) and the size and milling of the boards you want. Using your square footage figures and sketches, your dealer can compute the amount of material you need. Confirm that all undamaged and uncut materials can be returned to your dealer later for refund or credit.

If the wall you're paneling is a standard 8-foot height, and if you're using sheet paneling, figuring the number of panels you'll need is easy. Just measure the width of the wall in feet and divide by the width of your paneling. Round fractions off to the next largest number. The answer is the number of panels you need.

If your wall is taller than 8 feet, order extra-long panels or allow for extra panels to piece out the height. Chances are the seam between the two will be conspicuous, but it's easily covered with molding.

Unless a very large part of the wall is windows and doors, don't bother trying to deduct material for them. It's much easier during installation to cut window and door areas from whole sheets than to try to fit and piece around the openings.

If you're using sheet paneling and there's only bare studs in the area you're paneling, ask the dealer whether you'll need to back the material with gypsum board or other material for rigidity and fire protection. Building codes may require this, and if your dealer isn't thoroughly familiar with local codes, check with your building department.

CONDITIONING THE PANELING

Plan on storing all paneling in the room to be paneled for at least 2 days. This allows the paneling to adapt to the room temperature and humidity, preventing warping or buckling after installation. Stack paneling flat on the floor, separating each board or panel from the next by equivalent lengths of 2 by 4s or by furring strips.

If you can't stack paneling in the room to be paneled, place it off the floor in a well-ventilated room that has approximately the same temperature as the room to be paneled.

It's essential to keep board paneling in a dry place; otherwise, it will absorb moisture and warp. If there's a danger of moisture, cover the boards with plastic or another nonporous material, making sure it fits loosely around the wood to allow for air circulation.

If the room being paneled has a base of new plaster, wait until the plaster cures or apply a sealer before placing the paneling in the room. Plaster usually requires several days or more to cure, but you can often apply a primer sealer sooner than this. Paneling left in a freshly plastered room can absorb damaging moisture containing free lime, a caustic substance.

After the paneling has adapted to the room's conditions, stand the boards or panels side by side against the wall. Then step back and study the overall effect of the grain and coloring. Rearrange the boards or panels according to your preference, then mark the back of each according to this arrangement.

PREPARING THE SURFACE

Like painting, wallpapering, and most other interior finishing approaches, a successful paneling job requires careful preparation of the surface to be covered. Read the following sections carefully and complete the necessary preparations before you begin installing any paneling.

REMOVING MOLDING & BASEBOARDS

First, you'll need to remove all molding, baseboards, and "shoes" (usually oval-shaped strips on the baseboards). If you plan to reuse the molding material, be careful to avoid marring or splitting as you remove it.

Since most molding is attached with finishing nails, you have a choice of two ways to remove it.

One method is to hammer a thin, broad-bladed pry bar behind the molding and gently pry outward until the molding begins to give. Then move the bar over a few inches and repeat the process until the entire piece comes loose. Some nails will probably stay with the molding and others will pull through and remain sticking out of the wall. Using pliers, pull out the nails in the molding from the back side. Hammer in those nails remaining in the wall.

A second way to remove molding is to locate the nails and, using a nailset, drive each one all the way through the molding. After the molding is lifted off, pull out the nails. For hardwood moldings, this method is the best, but be careful not to crack the molding.

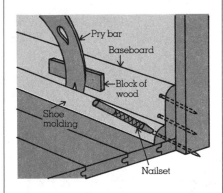

LOCATING & MARKING WALL STUDS

You'll have to locate the studs hidden within your present wall before you can attach the paneling. If you're installing furring strips first (see pages 88 and 89), you'll need to nail the strips to the studs through the wall's surface. If paneling is installed on the wall without furring, panels or boards are nailed directly to the studs through the wall.

Studs, vertical 2 x 4s, are normally spaced either 16 or 24 inches apart, center to center. They're nailed at the top and bottom of the wall frame to 2 by 4 horizontal plates (see page 84). At corners and around door and window frames, studs are usually doubled.

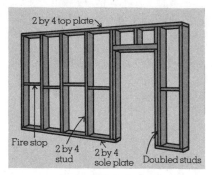

Anatomy of a typical wall

There are three methods for locating studs. As you find each one, mark it by snapping a chalk line (see page 51).

• Measure in 16 and 24 inches from each end of the wall. At those points, knock on the wall several times with your knuckles or the heel of your hand and listen closely. You'll

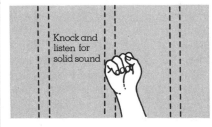

Knock and listen for solid sound

hear either a solid thud or a hollow sound. A thud means you've located a stud. A hollow sound indicates you should try again.

After you find the first stud, measure over 16 or 24 inches (the same as the distance from the corner to the first stud) to locate the next one.

• A second method is to use a magnetic stud finder, an inexpensive little tool with a magnetized needle that fluctuates when it passes over a nail head. If your existing wall covering is nailed to studs, the stud finder

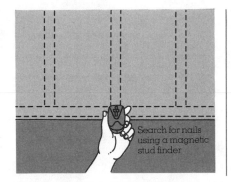

Search for nails using a magnetic stud finder

can help you locate the studs. It won't work on wall coverings attached with adhesive or where there's other metal beneath the wall's surface (like plaster over wire mesh).

● A third method is to probe into the wall about 2 inches above the floor using a long nail or drill. When you find a stud, measure 16 or 24 inches from that point to find the next stud.

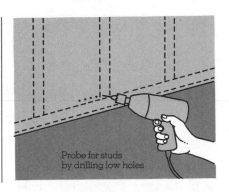

Probe for studs by drilling low holes

Helpful Paneling Tools

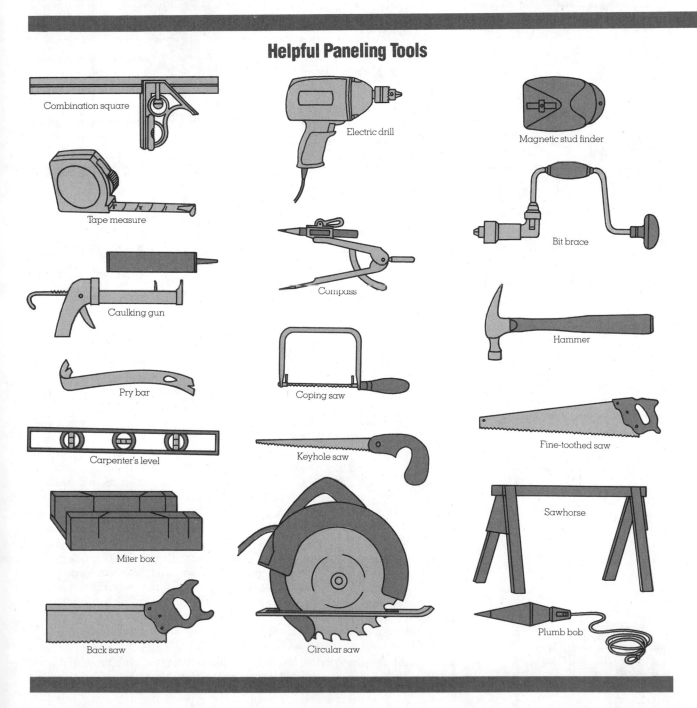

Combination square

Tape measure

Caulking gun

Pry bar

Carpenter's level

Miter box

Back saw

Electric drill

Compass

Coping saw

Keyhole saw

Circular saw

Magnetic stud finder

Bit brace

Hammer

Fine-toothed saw

Sawhorse

Plumb bob

INSPECTING THE SURFACE

It's essential to check the wall surface carefully to see if it's flat and plumb. If the surface of the wall is very bumpy or significantly out of plumb, you'll need to add furring strips (see facing page).

To check the surface for flatness, hold a long, straight 2 by 4 against the wall. (Don't use too short a straightedge—it won't adequately reveal irregularities.) Check the entire surface of the wall.

Then see if the wall is plumb. The easiest method is to hold a carpenter's level against the wall; the level's bubble should be properly framed between the hairlines. If you

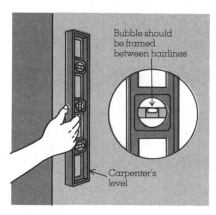

Bubble should be framed between hairlines

Carpenter's level

don't have a level, you can tack a plumb bob to the ceiling; when it hangs still, measure the distance from the wall to the string in several places. Move the plumb bob and repeat this procedure several more times. A plumb wall will show no variations.

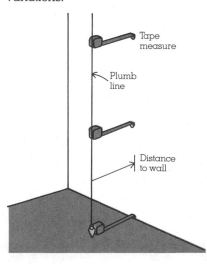

Tape measure

Plumb line

Distance to wall

If the wall is flat and plumb and you're using an adhesive, clean the wall with an ordinary household cleaner or a specialized wall cleaning product. Rinse the wall well and let it dry. Then use paneling adhesive to apply paneling directly to the surface (see the instructions beginning on page 92).

If the wall is plumb but a little bumpy or damaged, you can nail paneling directly to the wall, providing there are subsurface wooden studs, plates, and sills you can nail it to. Directions are on page 92.

FURRING & SHIMMING

Furring strips, usually 1 by 2s or 1 by 3s, are attached to a wall to provide a good nailing or gluing surface for paneling.

You'll need to install a framework of furring strips in these cases:

• if you're installing vertical solid board paneling;

• if your wall is very bumpy or severely damaged;

• if your wall is significantly out of plumb;

• if you need suitably spaced subsurface wall members for nailing;

• if you want to install insulation under the paneling.

The arrangement of the furring strips depends on the type of paneling being applied and, in the case of board paneling, its direction. Three arrangements are illustrated above right.

Keep in mind that a room isn't as stable as it appears to be; its floor and ceiling shift as the house settles. If you don't take this future shifting into account when you install rigid wall coverings, you can end up with buckled walls.

One way to avoid this is to leave a ½-inch space at the top and bottom of the wall when you're applying furring strips. Be sure to allow for this when you're measuring and cutting vertical strips.

To apply furring strips, follow the steps on the facing page. Always

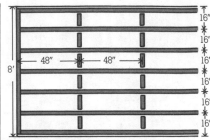

For 4 by 8 panels

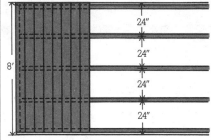

For vertical board paneling

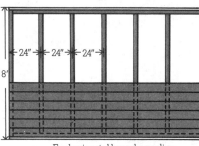

For horizontal board paneling

apply strips securely. For wooden walls, nails should penetrate at least 1 inch into the studs. For masonry walls, use concrete nails or expansion bolts.

Of course, furring strips should be plumb and flat. If the existing wall is severely out of plumb, you may need to taper the furring strips or block them out slightly at one end to provide a flat surface.

For minute adjustments, use shims. These are merely small wedges—usually shingles. When the furring is in place, check for flatness using a long straightedge (a short one won't reveal unevenness). Mark the areas of the furring that sag inward. These are the locations that need shims.

Simply tap them in place until the furring strips are flat and plumb; then tack the shims to the wall so they

How to Apply Furring Horizontally

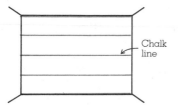 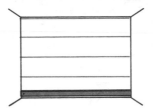 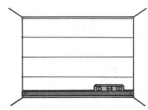

Step 1. Measure wall from corner to corner. For an 8-foot-high wall, cut 5 furring strips the same length as wall; for higher walls, add a furring strip for each additional 16 inches.

Step 2. Find and mark locations of wall studs across wall you intend to panel (see page 86). At a lower corner, nail one end of first strip to stud ½ inch up from floor, using one 10-penny nail.

Step 3. Placing a carpenter's level on opposite end of furring strip, raise strip until bubble in level is centered between hairlines. Then nail that end to a stud.

  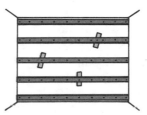

Step 4. Finish nailing furring strip to studs between corners, using one nail for each stud.

Step 5. To check for flatness, hold a long, straight 2 by 4 against furring strip. To make any necessary adjustments, shim furring strip out from wall until it's flat.

Step 6. Install remaining furring strips the same way, checking each one for level and flatness.

How to Apply Furring Vertically

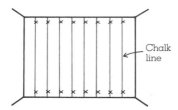 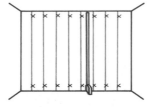 

Step 1. Find and mark locations of wall studs across wall you intend to panel (see page 86).

Step 2. Measure height from floor to ceiling along each stud mark and cut furring strips the length of wall's height minus 1 inch. Cut a furring strip for each stud.

Step 3. Allowing a ½-inch space at top and bottom, nail top of one furring strip to stud near corner of wall, using one 10-penny nail.

 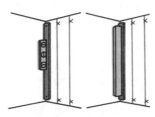 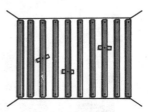

Step 4. Hold a carpenter's level against side of furring strip to check for plumb; if necessary, move it until plumb, then nail it to stud near floor.

Step 5. Use level to check front face for plumb; then hold a long, straight 2 by 4 against furring strip to check for flatness. To make any necessary adjustments, shim furring strip out from wall until it's flat.

Step 6. Install remaining furring strips the same way, checking each one for plumb and flatness.

won't fall out as you attach the paneling.

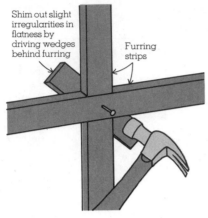

Shim out slight irregularities in flatness by driving wedges behind furring

Furring strips

When you add furring strips, you'll also need to adjust electric outlets, switches, and door and window frames to accommodate the increased wall thickness. Add your paneling's thickness to the furring's thickness—that's the distance you'll need to adjust outlets, switches, and frames out from their present positions.

To adjust door and window frames, you simply add material of sufficient thickness to the existing framework to accommodate the depth of furring and paneling. Take care to match surfaces so that painting will cover the joint between old and new material.

The illustration below shows a typical treatment for adjusting a window frame depth to match your new paneling. Use the same technique to prepare door frames.

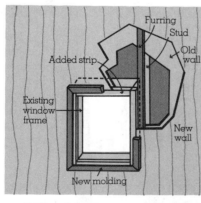

Furring
Stud
Old wall
Added strip
Existing window frame
New wall
New molding

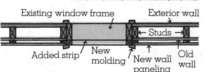

Existing window frame   Exterior wall
Studs
Added strip   New molding   New wall paneling   Old wall

Normally, electrical outlets and switch boxes are nailed to the side of a stud—usually toward the back. But sometimes they have a special flange by which they are nailed to the front of the stud. In this case, you'll have to cut away some gypsum board or plaster to pry them loose. *Caution:* Be sure to turn off the current before you move electrical outlets.

Older construction has metal boxes that require some effort to pry loose. Instead of trying to move the box, attach a metal extension sleeve (available at electrical supply stores) to the front of the box. Newer construction has plastic boxes with slanted nail guides that make them easier to remove and reinstall.

PREPARING PLASTER WALLS

You can install sheet or horizontal board paneling over plaster walls by driving nails through the paneling and plaster into the studs.

Since plaster walls are rarely plumb or square at top and bottom, you'll want to install furring strips first. In the long run, attaching furring strips is easier than sanding, patching, and sealing old plaster walls. And as an added advantage, furring provides a dead air space behind the panels, enhancing both sound and thermal insulation properties.

PREPARING MASONRY WALLS

Masonry walls present a special problem. Because of moisture condensation, you'll need to waterproof the walls before applying any covering to the surface.

If the concrete is new, it may contain mineral salts that are brought to the surface by water and appear as white deposits called efflorescence. These deposits will disappear once all the salts are leached out of the concrete, but the process can take years. Ask your paint or masonry dealer to recommend a waterproofing masonry sealer that blocks mineral salts.

Before sealing the surface, fill holes in concrete walls with cement grout. Spread it on smoothly and let it dry before applying the waterproofing sealer.

A vapor barrier paper or polyvinyl film used between the concrete and the furring strips will further minimize the possibility of moisture penetrating the paneling.

Attach furring to masonry, using expansion bolts.

If you're transforming a basement into a recreation room, you may want to create a basic framework of 2 by 4 studs to give enough depth for installing outlets and switches before you panel. In this case don't use furring strips; instead, place blocking between the studs to provide a nailing base.

INSTALLING YOUR PANELING

Whether you're using sheet paneling or solid boards, the basic installation techniques are the same. Careful measuring and precise cutting will ensure accurate, professional-looking results.

SHEET PANELING

Installing sheet paneling—from fitting the first panel to attaching panels securely to the wall surface—is exacting work, but it's not difficult. Before you begin, read through the following sections on cutting the panels and attaching them to the wall.

Whether you're nailing the panels to the surface or gluing them, be sure you've properly prepared the wall for the method you're using.

For appearance's sake, cut the first and last panels on the wall the same width, unless you're using panels with random-width grooves. Prop up all the panels along the wall to see how they'll fit. If the last panel has to be much narrower than the first one, cut both end panels to make them roughly equal in width.

Cutting panels

Before you begin cutting, check to see if the ceiling height varies. Then allow for a ½-inch clearance where the paneling joins the floor so the panels won't buckle as the house settles.

To avoid snapping a panel as you're sawing, support both halves on two or more sawhorses (or their equivalent); lay several furring strips or 2 by 4s across the horses for extra support.

Use a saw to cut wood and simulated-wood paneling materials. Choose a saw for fine cutting—10 to 15 teeth per blade inch. On both portable and bench-type power circular saws, use plywood-cutting blades.

Cut the panels *face up* if you're using a handsaw or table saw, *face down* with a portable circular or saber saw.

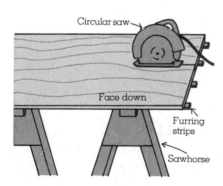

One way to avoid splintering the panel edges or tearing the veneer is to apply masking tape along the face of the cutting line. Be careful when removing the tape; its sticky side may be strong enough to splinter the wood. Another method is to use a sharp knife and straightedge to score the cutting line.

If you're using a handsaw, start the cut at the panel's edge; to score the panel, hold the saw's blade edge nearly level with the surface and use forward strokes only.

As you cut the panel, hold the

saw at a 30° angle. If it's hard to keep the saw on a straight line, clamp a straight board along the cutting line and let the saw ride against it.

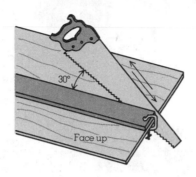

Scribing paneling. The first piece of paneling that you fit into the corner of a wall probably won't fit exactly the contours of the adjoining wall or floor. Nor is the paneling likely to be level or plumb. To duplicate the irregularities of the adjoining surface on the paneling's edge, use a compass or a scribing tool.

Prop the panel into place about an inch from the uneven adjoining surface; use shingles, if necessary, to shim the panel into level or plumb. Holding the compass's points parallel to each other, draw the compass along the surface so the pencil leg duplicates the unevenness onto the paneling.

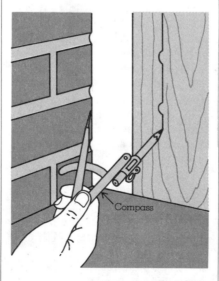

Cutting out doors, windows, and other openings. Fitting paneling around any opening requires careful measuring, marking, and cutting.

Before you measure for switches and outlets, remove their faceplates.

One way to measure and mark panels is to use a steel tape, keeping track of the measurements on a piece of paper. Starting from the corner of the wall or from the edge of the nearest panel, measure to the edge of the opening or outlet; then, starting at the same point, measure to the opening's opposite edge. Next, measure the distance from the floor to the opening's bottom edge and from the floor to the opening's top edge; remember that you'll install the paneling ½ inch up from the floor.

Marking the side of the panel that will face you as you cut (face up when using a handsaw, table saw, or keyhole saw, face down when using a portable circular saw or saber saw), transfer these measurements to the panel; be sure to measure from the correct edge of the panel. When marking the back of the panel, remember that measurements will be a mirror image of the opening.

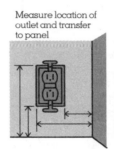

Measure location of outlet and transfer to panel

Drill holes in corners and cut opening

Face up

Another way to measure and mark panels for cutting is to make a template (see page 84) from the protective sheets that come with many manufactured panels. Because these sheets are the same size as the panels, you can tape one to the wall as though it were a panel. Mark the opening on the sheet or cut it out with a razor blade. Then lay the sheet on the panel; using the template as a pattern, mark the panel.

Cut large openings following the directions at left. To make cutouts in panels for small openings such as outlets and switches, drill holes in the panel in each of the corners of the opening you've marked. Then cut the opening, cutting from the front of the panel if you're using a keyhole saw, from the back when using a saber saw.

Attaching sheet paneling

When you're installing sheet paneling, whether you're using adhesive or nails, keep in mind that you must securely attach all edges of the paneling.

This is no problem when you're applying panels directly to a wall. Nor is it a problem when you apply panels to a framework of studs or furring strips spaced regularly at 16 or 24 inches, center to center—you butt the panels along the center of each framing member.

But if you're nailing directly to bare studs, you'll have to add 2 by 4 horizontal blocking (see page 88) between the studs to provide a nailing base for the edge of the paneling. Nail one block a quarter of the distance down from the top plate, one block halfway between floor and ceiling, and another block a quarter of the way up from the bottom plate.

Fastening with adhesives and nailing are the two basic methods for applying most sheet paneling. Using an adhesive is the favored method—it's fast and clean, and it doesn't subject panels to hammer dents or nail holes.

Adhesives. Follow the adhesive manufacturer's directions when you're applying paneling with an adhesive. Work with one panel at a time—don't apply adhesive beyond the area that one panel will cover.

Here's the typical procedure. On furring or exposed wall framing, apply adhesive to the framing in squiggly stripes; for direct-to-wall applications, apply in uniformly spaced stripes 12 or 16 inches apart.

Drive four 1¼-inch finishing nails through the top edge of the panel. Position it on the wall; drive the nails part way into the wall to act as hinge pins. Pull the panel's bottom edge about 6 inches out from the wall and push a block behind it to hold it

there; wait for the adhesive to get tacky—8 to 10 minutes.

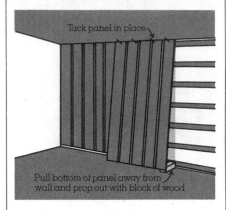

Tack panel in place

Pull bottom of panel away from wall and prop out with block of wood

Then, remove the block and press the panel firmly into place. To force the adhesive into tight contact, knock on the panel with a rubber mallet or hammer against a padded block. Be careful not to mar the surface.

Drive the nails at the top all the way in; then nail the panel at the bottom (you'll cover the nail heads later with molding). Thin paneling materials require either gluing or nailing within ½ inch of the edges of the paneling to prevent curling.

Nailing. When nailing the panels, be careful not to mar the surfaces. To keep nails as inconspicuous as possible, either use nails that are color-matched to your paneling or use finishing nails. Drive them into heavily textured areas or grooves where they'll be least noticeable. For lapped panels, drive nails through flanges.

If you want, use a nailset to recess the nail heads; then blend them to the surface, using a color-matched putty or repair stick.

Use 1¼-inch nails for panels less than ½ inch thick; for ⅝ or ¾-inch

panels, use 2-inch nails. Space them as shown in the illustration below.

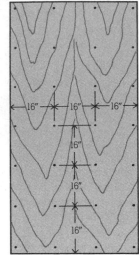

Proper nail placement for 4 by 8 panels

SOLID BOARD PANELING

Though solid boards are usually installed vertically or horizontally, you don't need to limit your options to these two installations. For an interesting effect, consider using a decorative pattern.

Cutting & installing boards

Instructions for cutting and installing boards in the various patterns begin on the facing page. You cut solid boards to fit into corners and around openings the same way as you do sheet paneling (see "Cutting panels," page 91). To prevent splintering, place finished boards *face up* if you're cutting them with a handsaw or a table saw, *face down* if you're using a portable circular or saber saw.

You can nail the boards to the wall surface or attach them with adhesive. Nailing is the preferred method. Use finishing nails and recess the heads ⅟₃₂ inch below the surface, using a nailset. Cover the nail heads, using a putty stick in a matching color.

Where you nail depends on the paneling's milling. Typical methods are shown above right.

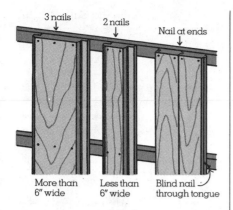

3 nails　2 nails　Nail at ends

More than　Less than　Blind nail
6" wide　6" wide　through tongue

Apply adhesives as described for sheet paneling (facing page), following the adhesive manufacturer's directions. Also nail the top and bottom of each board after gluing.

Patterns for solid board paneling

Follow the instructions that refer to the pattern you've chosen for your paneling.

Vertical pattern. Before paneling vertically with solid boards, you must attach horizontal furring strips (see pages 88–89).

Measure the width of the boards you're using, then measure the width of the wall. Using these figures, calculate the width of the final board. To avoid a sliver-size board, split the difference so the first and last boards are the same size.

When you place the first board into the corner, check the outer edge with a carpenter's level. If the board

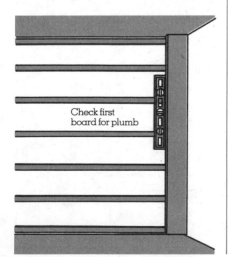

Check first board for plumb

isn't plumb or doesn't fit exactly against the adjoining wall, mark it (see "Scribing paneling," page 91). Then trim it, using a plane or saw.

Attach the first board; then butt the second board against its edge and check for plumb before you nail or glue it. Repeat this procedure for all subsequent boards.

Horizontal pattern. Generally, you won't need to apply furring unless the wall is badly damaged or not plumb. You can nail the boards to the studs through the wall covering. To avoid ending up with a very narrow board at the ceiling, work out and adjust its size as described under "Vertical pattern" (at left).

Start at a bottom corner of the wall and work up to the ceiling. Nail the first board temporarily at one end, ½ inch up from the floor. Then level the board and complete nailing. Attach the remaining boards in the same way.

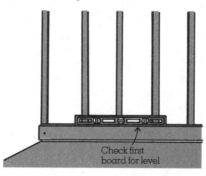

Check first board for level

Diagonal pattern. Installed correctly this pattern appears to run from one wall onto the next. For this reason, cutting the board ends requires special attention. Boards are usually installed at a 45° angle unless the

SHOP TALK

When you're installing solid board paneling across a wall, you may have trouble fitting the final board. To make this last board fit easily into place, cut its edges at a slight angle (about 5°) toward the board's back side.

room's shape or style suggests an alternative. Furring isn't needed unless the wall is badly damaged or not plumb.

If you're making end cuts at 45°, you'll need a combination square that has a 45° angle (if you're using a handsaw). Otherwise, a table (bench) or radial-arm saw will do it all very accurately with one adjustment.

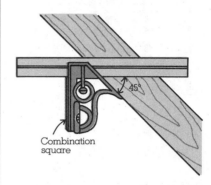

45°

Combination square

Where you begin installing the boards depends on whether you want the boards to run diagonally up to the right or left. If you start at the lower left corner, the boards will run up to the right. Start at the lower right corner to have the boards run up to the left.

In the corner where you want to begin, measure the height of the wall from floor to ceiling. Measure the same distance across the bottom of the wall and mark the wall at that point. Hang a plumb line (see page 42) directly above the mark and make another mark at the top of the wall. Using a straight board, draw a line from the bottom corner to the mark at the top of the wall. This line should form a 45° angle.

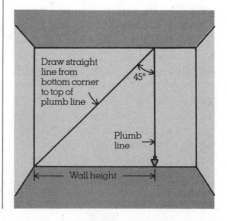

Draw straight line from bottom corner to top of plumb line

45°

Plumb line

Wall height

(Continued on next page)

PANELING　**93**

Measure the length of this line and transfer that measurement to a length of board paneling. Use a combination square to mark 45° end cuts if you're using a handsaw. Cut the board and nail or glue it into place. For each additional board,

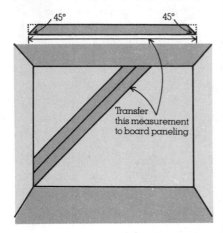

measure, mark, cut, and attach, using the same methods.

Herringbone pattern. Cutting the boards for this pattern requires even more care than for the diagonal pattern. And you may have to sand the cut ends lightly to make smooth joints.

As with the diagonal pattern, end cuts are usually made at a 45° angle. Furring isn't necessary because boards stretch across plates and studs and can be nailed directly to them.

Installing the boards in this pattern is a little tricky, but the final effect is well worth the effort. You start in one corner and work across the wall. You'll probably encounter the usual out-of-plumb condition at the starting corner. To ensure proper symmetry, use the following procedure.

Decide how many herringbones will make a pleasing pattern for the expanse of wall you want to panel. Make sure the center of each pattern falls on a stud.

Using a plumb line, mark the top and bottom of the wall over the center of a stud. Snap a chalk line (see page 51) between the marks or connect them using a straightedge. Each line will mark the center of a herringbone pattern.

Temporarily nail a 1 by 2 guide strip flush with the first chalk line. This strip provides a steady "third hand" as you lay up the first floor-to-ceiling half of a herringbone.

As you attach each board, rest one edge against the guide strip. This allows you to maintain plumb as you work upward.

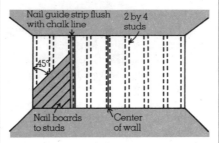

After you've installed a plumb half-herringbone, remove the guide strip; the completed half-herringbone will serve as a plumb guide for the rest of the job.

Random width and thickness pattern. You can install boards of varying widths, lengths, and thicknesses by nailing them against horizontal furring or by attaching them (usually with an adhesive) to sheets of inexpensive plywood. For this pattern, you can use pieces of scrap lumber, arranged in any order. Leave the surface natural or finish it with paint, primer, stain, or sealer.

Board and batten pattern. Install this pattern either vertically or horizontally (see page 93). For the vertical pattern, install furring.

Square-edge boards are the best choice for this pattern—tongue-and-groove or shiplap are unnecessary expenses.

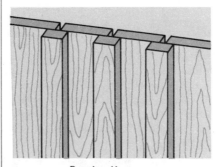

Board and batten

After installing the boards, simply nail battens (1 by 2-inch wood strips) over the seams where the boards meet.

Board on gap pattern. Install this pattern in the same way as you do vertical or horizontal patterns (see page 93). Each board is rabbeted—shiplap style—usually 1 inch at one side

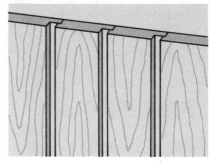

Board on gap

and ¼ inch at the opposite side. When two boards are butted together, you can see the ¾-inch groove between them.

Board on board pattern. Installation is the same as for board and batten (at left). Furring is necessary for ver-

Board on board

tical application. Space the boards several inches apart; then center and nail boards over the spaces.

Strip-facing pattern. Solid boards of the same or varying widths are separated by ¾-inch strips of 1 by 2 batten laid on edge. Because the boards are usually installed vertically, horizontal furring is required underneath.

Follow the installation instructions for vertical paneling (see page

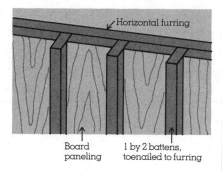

Horizontal furring

Board paneling

1 by 2 battens, toenailed to furring

93), but attach the 1 by 2 battens sideways so the 1-inch width faces the wall (see illustration above). Toe-nail the batten at each furring strip.

FINISHING TOUCHES

When your paneling is in place, all that remains is to add those small but important finishing touches. Molding not only covers exposed edges of paneling, but also adds character to your room when used decoratively. Most board paneling and some sheet paneling also require a stain or paint finish.

MOLDINGS

Moldings are more than a cover for the raw edges of wood paneling. You can use moldings to cover seams in sheet paneling, to camouflage mistakes and flaws, and to introduce architectural features that never existed before.

Molding along the bottom of the paneling will cover the ½-inch space between the paneling and the floor. You may also want to add molding at the ceiling line and along the edges of large openings, such as windows and doors. A common decorative use for molding is wainscoting (see page 84).

Moldings are available in a wide range of styles (see illustration above right) and in many materials, including milled wood, wood grain-printed plastic, vinyl, or aluminum. Most lumberyards carry a wide variety of molding strips to match what-

Inside cove   Stop   Corner   Crown

Shoe   Base   Cap   Casing

ever style of paneling you choose.

You can also use ordinary 1 by 2 battens as molding and 1 by 4 boards for baseboards, or you can even make your own molding.

Measuring and cutting molding. When measuring for molding—to frame a window, for example—measure the inside dimensions (see illustration below) and cut your material accordingly. Remember that you must reverse the cuts on the ends of each piece of molding.

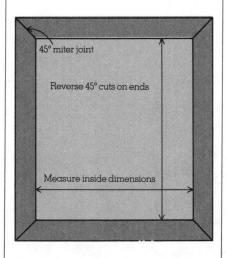

45° miter joint

Reverse 45° cuts on ends

Measure inside dimensions

Use a combination square for marking miter joints (see page 84). For cutting straight lines and miters accurately, use a miter box (see page 87) or a circular saw.

To fit curved moldings, such as

crown and base moldings, miter the ends or cut one end to the proper curvature. To cut a curved edge, use a coping saw.

Especially when it's curved, molding can be difficult to cut. Clamp the section you're working with so it won't "creep," but be careful to pad the material to avoid marring it. As in any other type of woodwork, remember that a saw blade has thickness, and allow for it.

Cut away the underside of the material when you're using thick molding so the outer (visible) edge of the molding will fit tightly.

Fastening molding. To attach molding, either nail it into place with finishing nails and recess the heads with a nailset, or blind nail the molding.

To blind nail, use a small knife or gouge to raise a sliver of wood that's large enough to hide the head of a finishing nail; don't break off the sliver. Pull the sliver to the side, nail into the cavity with a finishing nail, and then glue the sliver back into place.

You can tape the sliver down with masking tape until the glue is dry. Rubbing the spot lightly with fine sandpaper will remove all signs of fastening.

It's faster to make all the gouges first and then recess all the nails, rather than going through the entire procedure for one nail at a time.

FINISHING & MAINTAINING YOUR PANELING

Normal wear and tear in a home may leave walls with a deposit of dirt and grease that, if not regularly cleaned off, can gradually change the color of your paneling. For this reason, it's a good idea to apply a washable finish. If your paneling is unfinished, you can apply a penetrating stain or varnish. See the section on painting beginning on page 64.

Finished walls—either vinyl-covered sheet paneling or solid board paneling—should be waxed when first installed and then cleaned and rewaxed about twice a year.

INDEX

Boldface numbers refer to color photographs.